D1756106

# The Great Retreat of 1914
# From Mons to the Marne

Spencer Jones

© Spencer Jones 2014

Spencer Jones has asserted his rights under the Copyright, Design and Patents Act, 1988, to be identified as the author of this work.

First published by Endeavour Press Ltd. in 2014.

This edition published by Sharpe Books in 2018.

# Table of Contents

# Key Figures

**Britain**

Field Marshal Sir John French, Commander in Chief of the British Expeditionary Force

Lieutenant-General Sir Douglas Haig, Commanding I Corps

General Sir Horace Smith-Dorrien, Commanding II Corps

**France**

Marshal Joseph Joffre, Commander in Chief of the French Army

General Charles Lanrezac, Commanding French Fifth Army

**Germany**

Chief of the German General Staff, Helmuth von Moltke

General Alexander von Kluck, Commanding German First Army

General Karl von Bülow, Commanding German Second Army

# A Note on Name Conventions and Unit Sizes

To avoid confusion, all references to German units and formations will be rendered in italics. British and French units will retain standard font.

In 1914, a British infantry division had a paper strength of 18,073 all ranks and 5,592 horses, supported by 76 artillery pieces (54 x 18-pounders, 18 x 4.5-inch howitzers, and four 60-pounders) and 24 machine guns.

An individual infantry brigade numbered approximately 4,000 all ranks. Each brigade consisted of four battalions of 1,000 men. Each battalion was composed of four companies of 250 men each.

The British cavalry division of 1914 had a paper strength of 9,269 all ranks and 9,815 horses, supported by 24 13-pounder guns and 24 machine guns. An individual cavalry brigade numbered approximately 1,700 all ranks.

# Introduction: The Guns of August

In the swelteringly hot weeks of August 1914 the fate of Europe hung in the balance.

On 4 August, Germany hurled her forces into a carefully planned invasion of Belgium and France. The ambitious operation had first been proposed by Count Alfred von Schlieffen. Schlieffen had died in 1913 but his plan lived on.

The Schlieffen Plan was Germany's solution to the problem of a two-front war against France and Russia. Rather than split her forces and risk being defeated in detail, Germany planned to concentrate her strength in the west and land a knockout blow against France. If all went according to plan, the French would be defeated within six weeks, allowing Germany to transfer her armies to the eastern front and deal with Russia. German officers toasted to the success of the plan at the outbreak of war: 'Paris for lunch and St. Petersburg for dinner!'

The premise of the Schlieffen Plan was simple. Germany would take a defensive stance on the Franco-German border and use the formidable fortifications in the area to hold off the anticipated French offensives. Whilst the French were battering themselves to death on the frontier, the bulk of the German army would outflank them by invading neutral Belgium and using the country as a gateway to the heartlands of France. German spearheads would race south toward Paris like the sweep of a vast scythe, encircling the city and pinning the helpless French armies against the border, where they would be cut off and annihilated.

However, invading neutral Belgium carried serious consequences. Great Britain was bound, by the terms of an 1839 treaty, to protect Belgium from any invader. Furthermore, Britain was acutely aware of the dangers of allowing a hostile power to occupy the ports of Low Countries, which could then be used as a launch pad for an invasion of British Isles.

Germany knew that an attack on Belgium would bring Britain into the war. But the war planners dismissed the idea that this would interfere with the Schlieffen Plan. The British Expeditionary Force (BEF) numbered just 120,000 men and was dwarfed by the vast manpower of Germany. Kaiser Wilhelm II is said to have described the BEF as a: 'contemptible little army' and demanded that his men 'exterminate...the treacherous English.'

In numerical terms the British Expeditionary Force was certainly small – perhaps contemptibly so – but its size belied its fighting qualities. In contrast to the mass conscript armies of the continent, the BEF was a professional army consisting entirely of volunteers. As a result the force was, man for man, the best trained army in Europe. It was led by tough and experienced officers who had learned their trade in fierce colonial warfare. On hearing of the Kaiser's dismissive comments, the soldiers of the BEF began to refer to themselves as the Old Contemptibles. Their combat performance in 1914 would cement their place in history.

Within days of the BEF's deployment the full weight of the German invasion crashed into the thin British line. This book is the story of the Great Retreat that followed. Faced with overwhelming enemy numbers and battling alongside unreliable French allies, the BEF was forced to make an epic fighting withdrawal. The campaign was a battle for survival. Germany aimed to crush France in one fell swoop, whilst the Allies desperately sought time and space so that they could mount a counterattack to stem the tide.

There were moments on the Great Retreat when the fate of the BEF hung by the slenderest of threads. If the army had been wiped out then the history of Europe could have been very different. The destruction of Britain's only combat ready army would have been disastrous for the Allied war effort. It would have taken Britain months to replace the men and material lost in battle. During that time, France would have been left to fend off the German invasion alone and could well have been defeated. With France out of the war, Britain would have been a helpless spectator as Germany turned her victorious armies to crush Russia. Powerless to prevent the defeat of her continental allies, Britain would have been left with no option other than to sue for peace.

The stakes were high. Fortunately, the officers and men of the Old Contemptibles were up to the task. During the vicious rearguard battles of the Great Retreat, the BEF would prove to be the grit in the engine of the mighty German war machine. Ultimately, the withdrawal was successful and led directly to the decisive Allied counterattack at the Battle of the Marne, but only after a fortnight of ferocious combat, gruelling hardship and immense courage.

# Chapter 1: The British Army in 1914

## The Nature of the Army

Britain's official historian of the First World War, Brigadier-General James Edmonds, described the BEF of 1914 as: 'incomparably the best trained, best organised and best equipped British Army which ever went forth to war.' Edmonds had served as a staff officer in 4th Division in 1914 and had a nostalgic affection for the pre-war army which may have coloured his views. Nevertheless, although criticised on points of detail, historians have generally agreed with Edmonds's interpretation, particularly regarding the standard of training in the British Army.

The BEF was noted for its advanced tactics. The army owed much of its skill to the bitter experience of the Boer War (1899-1902). In 1899 the British government, wishing to annex the small Boer republics of South Africa to acquire their substantial gold and diamond reserves, had provoked war in anticipation of an easy victory. The conflict seemed a mismatch. The British Empire was the largest, richest and most powerful in the world. By contrast the Boers lacked a formal army and instead relied upon a citizen militia that was called together in times of emergency. But the war confounded expectations. Although they were civilians, the Boers were hardy frontiersmen. Mounted on rugged South African ponies,

15

the Boers were crack shots and understood the terrain. They soon adopted guerrilla tactics and proved to be resilient, resourceful and exceptionally tough opponents. Sheer attrition eventually ground the Boers down, but by the end of the war in 1902 the British had suffered almost 100,000 casualties. A testament to the toughness of the Boers is the fact that Winston Churchill adopted the Boer word for their military units – 'commando' – and used it as the title of Britain's elite Special Forces in the Second World War.

Rudyard Kipling described the Boer War as 'no end of a lesson' for Britain and her army. Fortunately, the lessons of the conflict were absorbed. The war had revealed the importance of firepower, the need for initiative and flexibility in battle, and the necessity of improved weaponry. Between 1902 and 1914 the army overhauled its tactics, training and equipment to take account of its experiences. The process was still on-going in 1914 but it had already produced impressive results. Observing training exercises in 1913, a French officer praised British tactics, noting that attacks were 'carried out in an excellent manner...Infantry makes wonderful use of the ground, advances, as a rule, by short rushes and always at the double, and almost invariably fires from the prone position.'

A defining feature of British tactics was the emphasis on marksmanship. Following the painful experience of being outclassed by Boer marksmen in South Africa, the army had placed a premium on turning its soldiers into first class shots. From 1902 to 1914 the British allocated at least 250 rounds per man for musketry practice each year, the highest amount of any army in the world. Both infantry and cavalry completed the same marksmanship course as, uniquely amongst the armies of Europe, the British expected their cavalry to be as proficient in dismounted fighting as they were in the traditional mounted role.

The culmination of annual rifle training was the legendary 'mad minute' exercise in which a soldier was required to fire 15 shots in 60 seconds at a target 300 yards away. To increase the difficulty, the man was only allowed to begin with 5 rounds in the rifle, and was only permitted to reload in 5 round increments thereafter. Passing this exercise was considered the true mark of a soldier and experienced men were capable of scoring 20 or more hits within the minute. In 1914 the army record stood at an astounding 38 rounds in 60 seconds, with every shot hitting the inner ring of the target.

The army responded enthusiastically to the training. Many soldiers spent their spare time practicing so that they could achieve better scores on the shooting range. Those who reached high standards were rewarded with increased pay and coveted marksman badges. There was fierce competition amongst the men to be rated as the best 'shooter' in the company. By 1914 the most prestigious marksmanship competitions were attracting so many entrants that they were in danger of becoming unmanageable.

But the BEF had one serious weakness: its size. From 1902 to 1914 the army had worked within a very tight budget and laboured under the constant fear of spending cuts. This had gravely limited the size of the force and the BEF's fighting establishment was just 120,000 men. More worryingly, there were limited reserves available

17

to replace losses. Replacements for casualties could be sourced, to an extent, from regular units stationed in India and other parts of the Empire. However, this would take time and there was no immediate prospect of reinforcement. In theory, the regulars would be reinforced by the Territorial Army, which had been established in 1908 to provide a 'second line' for the BEF. However, the Territorials were part time soldiers and would need at least six months' additional training before they were considered ready for action. For the opening weeks of the war the regulars of the BEF would have to shoulder the strain alone.

The budget constraints that had limited the size of the army had also shaped its equipment. The army had taken advantage of the political shockwaves created by the Boer War to persuade the government to fund the purchase of new weaponry, but as the dust settled the Treasury reverted to its normal parsimonious stance. The Army possessed much fine equipment – the Lee-Enfield carried by infantry and cavalry was considered by many to be the best bolt action rifle in the world, and the 18-pounder guns of the Royal Artillery would prove their worth – but the Treasury frowned on requests for additional material. Appeals for extra machine guns and advanced automatic rifles were declined largely on financial grounds. As a result the British Army went to war in 1914 with two machine guns per battalion, a figure which compared most unfavourably to the plentifully supplied Germans.

The BEF was thus highly trained, tactically elite and in some ways well equipped. But it had distinctly limited supplies of trained manpower and was short of heavy weapons. It would fall to the fighting skills of the soldiers to make up for any deficiencies.

## The Battalion

At the heart of the British Army lay the battalion system. In 1914 there were still some older officers who remembered the upheavals of the 1880s when the battalions had lost their numerical designations and been given regional associations. The immense controversies surrounding this decision had long since faded, although some regiments clung to their old numerals, such as the Oxfordshire and Buckinghamshire Light Infantry which still proudly referred to itself as the 52nd Light Infantry.

The fierce loyalty held by soldiers to their battalion can seem strange to a modern audience reading at a time when most of the famous regiments of 1914 have vanished into amalgamations. Even at the time, the devotion British soldiers had for their battalion was largely incomprehensible to foreign observers, who felt that the men's loyalty should lie with their nation. But the battalion provided something far more tangible than the abstract concept of national identity. The battalion was both a 'home' and a 'team' for the men. They came to respect their officers and formed deep friendships with their comrades. The sense of belonging was enhanced by the battle history of the battalion which provided a unique identity and an inspirational example.

This bonding process was especially important because the pre-war Army recruited primarily from the poorest areas of the country. In the Edwardian era the phrase 'it's the workhouse or the army' was

19

analogous to 'between the Devil and the deep blue sea'. Many desperate men joined the military to avoid starvation. In 1913 less than 50% of enlistments had any form of trade. Therefore the battalion system gave a sense of belonging to some of the poorest and worst educated of society. In the words of historian Richard Holmes, it 'bestowed an expectation of courage' and provided 'something to look up to, something to admire, even something to worship.'

Battalions were ranked by the loosely defined concept of 'smartness'. The date which a unit had been founded played a part in this ranking system, but many other factors were taken into consideration. By virtue of their age, royal connections and impressive appearance the cavalry regiments and Guards battalions were at the top, closely followed by fashionable line formations such as the Queen's (Royal West Surrey Regiment) and the Northumberland Fusiliers. Regiments that were not considered 'smart' strove to enhance their status, usually by gaining a reputation for military prowess, particularly marksmanship, or through sporting achievements. Rivalry between battalions was fierce and sometimes disruptive, but the army took the view that there was no harm in it as long as it enhanced soldierly pride and boosted morale.

Field Marshal Bill Slim, a junior officer in the First World War who rose to command 14th Army in Burma in the Second World War, commented that the battalion system is 'the foundation of the British soldier's stubborn valour'. On the Great Retreat battalion loyalty and the fear of letting down comrades helped to sustain men in the face of confusion, hunger and exhaustion.

## Reserves

There was one weakness in the battalion system. The units were almost never at full strength. A combination of limited recruitment, budget restrictions, and the need to send drafts to the garrisons of India and the Empire all conspired to keep most of the home battalions well below their paper strength of 1,000 men.

In the event of war the shortfall was to be made good by recalling the reserves. There were two types of reservist in 1914. The most numerous were those men who had completed their service with the army and returned to civilian life. These ex-soldiers were paid a small wage for remaining in the reserves and in return were required to attend 12 training days a year, with the time there spent mainly on marksmanship. A second, smaller pool of soldiers was provided by the Special Reserve which was comprised of men who wished to serve but who could not commit to an army career. The Special Reserve trained full time for six months on enlistment and then four to six weeks a year thereafter.

In August 1914 the reserves were recalled to bring the battalions up to strength. Although the reservists were enthusiastic they lacked recent military experience. Long practiced skills such as marksmanship returned quickly, but physical fitness took longer. A sergeant of the 2nd Royal Welch Fusiliers recalled: 'There was no need to ask who was a Reservist, his white skin distinguished him from the tanned, fit serving man'. The lack of fitness was

21

compounded by the fact that the reservists were issued with new, unbroken boots on arrival at the battalion. These twin factors would have debilitating effects during the gruelling marches of the Great Retreat.

## Command and Leadership

A striking feature of the BEF was the wide range of combat experience possessed by both junior and senior officers. Officers proudly wore medals won during campaigns in South Africa, the Sudan, and Afghanistan, amongst many others. Although colonial combat was very different to full scale European warfare, its value should not be underestimated. Imperial conflicts were an unforgiving school for British officers, brutally rooting out the incompetent and the inefficient. It was a tough proving ground and several officers went to war in 1914 carrying scars from wounds suffered in colonial actions, but it provided priceless experience of leading men in battle. Leadership qualities of courage, tenacity and quick decision making were essential in 'small wars' and would prove invaluable on the Great Retreat.

In addition to their experience, most British officers took pride in being fit and hard. The popular pastimes of horse riding, hunting and polo all contributed to a high standard of fitness, as did long distance cycling, a sport which had become fashionable in the years just before the war. Officers who were overweight or unfit were frowned upon by their peers and quietly mocked by their men. The importance of physically fit officers would be proven beyond doubt on the Great Retreat.

Overall, there is little doubt that the front line officers of the BEF – from lieutenant to colonel – were highly competent. Experienced in small wars, hardened by active lifestyles and dedicated to their battalion, they formed an essential backbone of leadership in the Great Retreat.

Conversely, the actions of the senior officers on campaign would prove controversial. The commanders of the BEF were highly experienced men of marked personality and strong opinions. In the small world of the regular army it was inevitable that this would produce friction. Historian Stephen Badsey has compared the higher command of the British Army of 1914 to a modern parliamentary party: broadly united behind its leader, but coloured by an ever changing mosaic of official and unofficial alliances and cliques.

The Commander-in-Chief of the BEF was Field Marshal Sir John French. French had a reputation as a forward thinking officer and had made his name commanding the Cavalry Division in South Africa. He was considered a 'soldier's general', charismatic, courageous and much loved by his troops. However, there were question marks over his suitability to command the army in battle. French was a fiery character, possessing a 'mercurial' temperament that veered from wild optimism to deep pessimism and back again. This made it almost impossible for him to take a cool, considered view of the campaign and as a result he frequently failed to understand the situation facing his army.

Directly beneath French in the chain of command were the corps commanders Lieutenant-General Sir Douglas Haig and General Sir

Horace Smith-Dorrien, who took charge of I and II Corps respectively. French thought very highly of Haig. The two had served together in the Boer War and both shared a cavalry background and similar views on the tactics of the mounted arm. More practically, Haig had once provided a substantial loan to French so that the latter could pay off debts. Haig was considered one of the brightest stars in the British Army and much was expected from him in war. A handsome, taciturn Scotsman, he had played a leading role in creating the British Army's doctrine before the First World War. Haig was head of the prestigious Aldershot Command in 1914 and the units stationed here were converted into I Corps at the outbreak of hostilities. This gave Haig the advantage of going to war alongside officers and units that he already knew. Some of the 'smartest' battalions of the army were in I Corps and it was considered an elite formation.

However, Haig felt the weight of responsibility acutely in August 1914 and his performance proved controversial in some respects, although he retained French's approval. However, unbeknownst to the commander in chief, Haig harboured a low opinion of Sir John's generalship. Haig recorded his contempt for French in his diary and forwarded highly critical letters to senior figures in the British establishment. This would not become public knowledge until after the war.

Conversely, there was no secret about French's relationship with Sir Horace Smith-Dorrien. Their prolonged and bitter pre-war feud was the stuff of army legend. The two had clashed spectacularly

24

during a dispute over cavalry tactics in 1909 and were barely on speaking terms in 1914. Smith-Dorrien was a last minute addition to the commanders of the BEF, replacing the unfortunate Lieutenant-General Sir James Grierson after the latter had died of a sudden heart attack on 17 August. French had opposed the appointment but had been overruled by the Secretary of State for War, Lord Kitchener.

Smith-Dorrien was a talented general who had the most combat experience of any of the senior officers of the BEF. His fighting career had begun at the Battle of Isandlwana (1879), when he was one of just five officers to survive the disastrous defeat at the hands of the Zulus, and he had seen action in Egypt, Sudan, India and South Africa. He had a practical and hard bitten outlook on war and whilst he was noted for being intensely loyal to his subordinates, he did not suffer fools gladly. He was notorious for his temper and his rage was considered to be most terrifying in the entire army. His temperament was volcanic – one moment completely calm, the next erupting with fury. Fortunately for the BEF, Smith-Dorrien was also a skilful commander who swiftly earned the respect and trust of his men. As will be seen, his talents would play a vital role on the Great Retreat.

Aside from their strained interpersonal relationships, the greatest challenge facing French and his corps commanders was inexperience in handling large formations. French had commanded a cavalry division of approximately 9,000 soldiers in 1900, but in 1914 he was expected to control an army of 120,000 men. Haig and Smith-Dorrien were similarly inexperienced. Peacetime manoeuvres in which senior officers commanded their formations against one another had attempted to address the problem, but there was a world of difference between the 'sham fights' of training and the reality of combat. The commanders of the BEF were forced to learn in the field. Their success – or otherwise – would make the difference between victory and defeat.

*

Although thoroughly trained, well led and highly motivated, the BEF of 1914 was a small and, by virtue of its limited ability to replace losses, somewhat fragile instrument. It was aptly described as a 'rapier amongst scythes' by historian Basil Liddell Hart: a small and deadly weapon if handled deftly, but at risk of being broken by the sheer weight of its opponent's blows. This placed pressure on Sir John French and his subordinates to command the army with skill, ensuring that its strengths were emphasised and weaknesses minimised. The risks were acute. The BEF was Britain's only battle ready army and if it was wiped out then the consequences would be disastrous.

# Chapter 2: Advance to Contact

Responding to the German invasion of Belgium, Britain declared war on Germany on 4 August 1914. Within hours the army had begun its mobilisation – recalling reservists, assembling stores, distributing maps and requisitioning trains to take the soldiers to the coast for embarkation. By 17 August the majority of the BEF had arrived in France. It consisted of I Corps (1st Division and 2nd Division), II Corps (3rd Division and 5th Division), the Cavalry Division, plus two independent brigades in the form of 19th [Infantry] Brigade and 5th Cavalry Brigade. Two army divisions, 4th Division and 6th Division, were retained in Britain to protect the country against any attempt by the Germans to mount a surprise invasion.

The BEF was very much a junior partner to the vast French army and Sir John was expected to cooperate and coordinate with his allies, although he was not formally required to do so. The French, ignorant of the Schlieffen Plan, had begun the war with an all out offensive into the border provinces of Alsace-Lorraine. This territory had been part of France until it was annexed by Germany following the Franco-Prussian War (1870-71). French national pride demanded its recapture and Commander-in-Chief Marshall Joseph Joffre was convinced that the war would be won on this front.

There was no obvious place for the BEF in the frontier battles, and so the British Army was assigned a minor role on the far left flank, operating between Mauberge and Le Cateau. This position suited Sir John. It kept the BEF relatively close to the Channel ports on which the army depended for supplies and also allowed the British to advance northeast to the aid of the beleaguered Belgians. However, there were also weaknesses with this location. Operating at the far end of the French line meant that the BEF's left flank was open and virtually unprotected, screened only by French territorial troops of uncertain quality.

On the right flank was French Fifth Army, a large and powerful formation consisting of five infantry corps and a corps of cavalry. Fifth Army was due to advance into southern Belgium to attack German forces and would thus be fighting alongside the British in the coming campaign. Shared objectives suggested rich opportunities for cooperation. Unfortunately, the commander of Fifth Army, General Charles Lanrezac, took a different view. Lanrezac was an acerbic, pessimistic officer who held a low opinion of the British Army and spoke no English. Lieutenant Edward Spears, a BEF liaison officer, described him as 'a big flabby man with an emphatic corporation' who had the strange habit of removing his spectacles and hooking them over his right ear.

On 17 August Sir John French travelled to Lanrezac's headquarters to discuss Allied operations. The meeting was an utter disaster. Lanrezac greeted Sir John with the blunt comment: 'Well here you are. It is just about time. If we are beaten it is thanks to you.' Recovering from this brusque introduction, Sir John attempted to address the assembled officers in French but stumbled over his pronunciation. Lanrezac openly mocked his British counterpart for this gaffe and treated the rest of the meeting as a tiresome inconvenience. No plans were made for cooperation. Lanrezac flatly informed French that he would be attacking and that it was up to the BEF to keep up and maintain its position on the left flank.

By the time the ill-starred meeting ended the Allied commanders had come to despise one another. Lanrezac felt that Sir John was ignorant and stupid. French thought that Lanrezac was a 'pedant' whose 'superior education had given him little idea of how to conduct a war'. The dismal state of Anglo-French relations would make the coming campaign all the more difficult.

This inauspicious start was compounded by the lack of clear information about the strength and location of German forces operating in Belgium. Sir John scribbled in his diary: 'The fog of war hangs heavily over us'. The poor state of Allied cooperation meant that the French were slow to inform the British of events elsewhere on the front. Disquieting rumours of French defeats trickled into British General Headquarters (GHQ) but were discounted by the optimistic Sir John. Worse, the true scope of the German invasion of Belgium was not yet understood. Lacking information to prove otherwise, French assumed that the British advance towards Brussels would only be opposed by light forces. In fact, the BEF would be advancing into the teeth of General

Alexander von Kluck's mighty *First Army*, a formation that outnumbered the British by more than 3 to 1.

The Allies marched into Belgium with great confidence, but British reconnaissance soon began to paint a disturbing picture. Aircraft observed large German columns on the march and Brigadier-General David Henderson, the commander of the Royal Flying Corps, considered one such report so important that he delivered it to GHQ personally. Meanwhile, the advanced British cavalry screen found itself skirmishing with approaching German horsemen. The BEF's first shots of the war were fired on 22 August when a squadron of the 4th Dragoon Guards routed a German cavalry patrol. Remarkably, GHQ refused to grasp the true implications of these reports.

But events were moving fast. On the evening of 22 August, the intrepid Lieutenant Spears arrived at GHQ with the alarming news that Lanrezac had been defeated at the Battle of Charleroi and was falling back. The sudden retreat of Fifth Army left the BEF isolated and facing a German advance of unknown strength. Having spent the previous week full of optimism, Sir John was stunned by the news and slow to react. The situation was further complicated when a French officer arrived late that night with a request for the British to attack and relieve the pressure on Lanrezac's retreating troops. Lacking clear information of enemy dispositions, any such attack would be a blind leap of faith and Sir John declined the request. Instead, he made the fateful decision to hold the BEF in its current position for 24 hours to secure the left flank of Fifth Army.

This decision has puzzled historians. The BEF's own flanks were open and unprotected, the strength of the German opposition was unclear, and a delay of a day would widen the gap between the British and the retreating French. Some authors have seen Sir John's stand as a courageous and honourable action to assist his ally, but others have seen it as military folly influenced by his optimistic belief that he would still be able to launch an offensive towards Brussels. What seems certain is that French underestimated the scale of the German assault that was about to strike his army.

Whatever the case, Sir John's mind was clearly clouded as he ordered his army to prepare for battle. The BEF had finished the day's march at the Belgian mining town of Mons. At 5.30am French called a command conference where he ordered Haig and Smith-Dorrien to take positions in and around the town. French's instructions were vague, but when Smith-Dorrien asked if he was to defend the position or use it as a jumping off point for an attack he was brusquely told to stop asking questions. After giving his orders, Sir John made the odd decision to leave the area, driving to Valenciennes to inspect a new infantry brigade before leisurely returning to GHQ at Le Cateau in the afternoon. He would play no role in the battle on the 23 August.

Meanwhile, the powerful forces of the German *First Army* were advancing on the British position. The stage was set for the BEF's baptism of fire.

# Chapter 3: The Battle of Mons

## The British Position

The British did not consider Mons an attractive town. James Edmonds left an evocative description: 'one huge unsightly village, traversed by a vast number of devious cobbled roads which lead from no particular starting-point to no particular destination, and broken by pit-heads and great slag-heaps, often over a hundred feet high.' Infantryman Jim Cannon remembered: 'I took one look at it and thought what a bloody place to live. I took a second look and thought what a bloody place to fight.' The town was bisected by a broad canal. This terrain feature would shape the fighting.

I Corps took position on the right flank of the army and was virtually unengaged during the battle. Conversely, the duty of covering the canal fell to II Corps and this formation would bear the brunt of the fighting. Smith-Dorrien was a hardened veteran and he knew a bad position when he saw it. The canal was difficult to defend. It was crossed by no less than 18 bridges, and there was not enough time or explosives to demolish them all. The north bank was lined with trees and houses that the Germans could use as cover as they approached. On the British side, the built up environment made it almost impossible to deploy artillery support and the maze of streets created problems when moving up reinforcements or evacuating casualties. Smith-Dorrien asked for permission to withdraw from the canal and take up a superior position further south, but the request was denied.

At the front line the soldiers prepared themselves as best they could. Trenches were dug where the ground permitted, machine guns were emplaced to sweep the bridges with fire, street barricades were erected to block key roads, and buildings were loop-holed to serve as strong points. The Royal Artillery managed to drag some 18-pounder guns onto the canal tow path to provide heavy fire support. Ambush parties were sent to the northern bank to intercept German scouts and keep the enemy blind.

August 23rd dawned with light showery rain, but this soon gave way to blue skies and scorching sun. There was no breeze to relieve the sweltering temperatures. In places artillery observers climbed large slag heaps for a better view of the approaching Germans, but the heat of the day meant that the surface of the mound was soon unbearably hot. One gunner remembered 'within a couple of minutes our boots were sizzling, and down we came.'

An illusion of peace hung over the town. Belgian civilians went about their business, apparently unaware that a major battle was imminent. Captain Tudor St. John of the Northumberland Fusiliers recalled how efforts to create a barricade were impeded: 'We were much hindered by the crowds of curious sightseers who looked on with amazed delight at the unusual sight of strangely garbed soldiers destroying someone else's property and now and then I had to use sufficiently strong measures to scatter them to permit the men to work.' Elsewhere Private Sidney Godley of the 4th Royal Fusiliers remembered he was manning his machine gun position when 'a little boy and girl came up and brought me some rolls and coffee.' Soon after the fighting began, Godley warned the children: 'You'd better sling your hooks now, otherwise you may get hurt.'

To the north, the news that the British were blocking the way ahead came as a great surprise to von Kluck and *First Army*. German officer Walter Bloem remembered that the first he knew of it was 'when two Hussars, covered in blood, galloped up to us stating that the enemy was holding the line of the canal in front.' Although ignorant of the numbers or exact position of the BEF, the Germans immediately advanced to attack. With *First Army* wheeling to the south, the attack took the form of a rolling series of assaults, starting on the right of II Corps and gradually spreading westwards as more and more German units arrived on the field.

The Germans had numbers on their side, advancing with eight divisions against the BEF's four and ultimately concentrating six divisions against the two of II Corps. The British had an edge in training and held the advantage of occupying a defensive position. The Battle of Mons was about to begin.

### The Battle

The first shots of the battle were fired on the northern bank as the ambush parties carried out their lethal work. Soon these men were hurrying back across the bridges to warn their comrades that a major attack was imminent. However, it was the German artillery that began the action in earnest, sending shrapnel and high explosive

34

shells plunging into the buildings on the south side of the canal. Their fire was sporadic and inaccurate at first. However it was enough to send civilians fleeing from the streets, leaving the town eerily empty. Curtains twitched as locals nervously watched the proceedings from their houses. In contrast, the men of the 2nd Royal Irish Rifles greeted the inaccurate fire with bravado. Corporal John Lucy recalled: 'Some [men] laughingly...shouted advice to the German gunners: "Washout", "Another miss", and "Lower your sights."' One wag, simulating great terror, cried: 'Send for the police, there's going to be a row on here'. But soon the Germans found the range and the laughter abruptly ceased as the men dived for cover. Casualties followed. A Gordon Highlander recalled: 'God! How their artillery do fire...All at once, so it seemed, the sky began to rain down bullets and shells.' Although the bombardment was desultory compared to the storms of steel that would later characterise the Western Front, it was frightening enough for the troops under fire.

Soon, a new sound became discernible over the din of the bombardment. The 'conch like' calls of German bugles heralded the arrival of enemy infantry. Uncertain of what lay ahead of them and perhaps believing they were only opposed by a screen of dismounted cavalry, the German infantry rushed to the attack. To the amazement of the British, the first German units on the field advanced in old fashioned 'Prussian Drill' formations, lines of men shoulder to shoulder, led by officers with swords drawn. There is a certain element of controversy about this opening attack and German sources published after the war do not make mention of such formations, but evidence from British eyewitnesses is virtually unanimous.

The tightly packed assault lines offered a perfect target for British rifle fire. An infantryman remembered the electrifying call of whistle blasts signalling 'rapid fire' and the roar of musketry that followed as 'the most exhilarating sound I ever heard.' The results were devastating. A Gordon Highlander recalled that the first waves of attackers 'were simply blasted away to Heaven'. John Lucy wrote: 'For us the battle took the form of well-ordered rapid rifle-fire at close range, as the field-grey human targets appeared, or were struck down...Our rapid fire was appalling even to us...[and] after the first shock of seeing men slowly and helplessly falling down as they were hit, gave us a great sense of power and pleasure.' An officer commanding a machine gun of the King's Own Scottish Borderers recalled: 'This was our first experience of killing people: it was rather horrible, but satisfactory'. Elsewhere, the British put what they had learned in South Africa to good use. A sergeant of the 1st Lincolnshire Regiment recalled ordering his best marksmen to use independent fire to pick off officers and signallers, remembering: 'That is another trick taught to us by Brother Boer, and our Germans did not like it at all.'

Walter Bloem experienced the effects of this fire first hand, writing that: 'it was as if the hounds of hell had been loosed at us, yelling, barking, hammering as a mass of lead swept in among us.' The experience was the same across the front. Lashed by a storm of

36

bullets, German infantry reeled away in confusion, leaving behind scores of dead and wounded men. The survivors disappeared into the plentiful cover on the northern side of the canal. All assumptions that the position was lightly defended had been abruptly dispelled. A lull followed whilst the bloodied attackers regrouped and reinforcements assembled. Stung by their initial experiences, renewed attacks were made in extended lines. Small groups dashed forward under covering fire and tried to worm their way ever closer to the bridges. The Germans aimed to suppress the defenders long enough to allow assault parties to cross to the southern side of the canal.

The terms of the engagement were set. Close range fire fights raged around the bridges. German machine guns began to deploy alongside the infantry and the distinctive chatter of these weapons added to the deafening roar of battle. Artillery continued to pound the southern bank. Shrapnel bursts left behind clouds of greyish smoke that lingered in the still air, whilst high explosive rounds tore apart buildings and started fires. Bullets struck walls and ricocheted over the heads of crouching soldiers. Whistle blasts and bugle calls pierced the air. The Germans made several attempts to storm the crossing points, but all attacks were driven back by ferocious British fire, leaving the bridges littered with bodies.

But the attackers soon discovered a weak link in the British line. The bend of the canal formed an unfortunate salient at the Nimy rail bridge. This position was held by the 4th Royal Fusiliers and the 4th Middlesex. Both battalions came under ferocious attack. Engaged from the front and enfiladed from the flanks, the salient became an inferno and British casualties rapidly mounted. By early afternoon the position was judged to be untenable and orders were given for the battalions to fall back. The retirement was covered by machine gun fire from Lieutenant Maurice Dease and Private Sidney Godley. Dease was killed and Godley seriously injured and taken prisoner, but their sacrifice allowed their comrades to withdraw. Both men were awarded the Victoria Cross. The retreat of the Middlesex was covered by the actions of a single unknown rifleman, who climbed onto the roof of a train station and picked off approaching Germans until he was finally killed.

However, the retreat of the two battalions allowed the Germans to secure a bridgehead over the canal. The situation worsened as German units slipped across further to the east where the canal was only covered by a thin outpost line. These infiltrators began to advance through the town with the intention of cutting off British defenders at the bridges. Their movement was brought to a halt by the 1st Gordon Highlanders and 2nd Royal Scots, but the Germans fed in reinforcements and soon the Scottish battalions were under severe pressure. The battle on the flank turned into 'thoroughly unpleasant' street fighting, with soldiers firing at one another from windows, behind lampposts and around street corners.

Civilians were caught in the crossfire. After crossing the bridge at Nimy, German troops evicted a number of locals from nearby houses and used them as human shields to cover their advance. In the confused fighting that followed, seven of the civilians were killed and several others wounded. On another part of the front Captain St.

John recalled: '3 or 4 little girls dashed out of a house. They went across the street into another house and then back again and then backwards and forwards once more. I called out to cease fire, which was done at once. The lull only lasted for 2 or 3 minutes during which time I could hear these children crying but it was long enough to enable the Germans to cut some of my barbed wire and get round to the coal sheds to our west.' St. John was convinced that the Germans had driven the children onto the street deliberately, but it may have been an unfortunate coincidence.

Fierce street fighting raged throughout the afternoon until the battle petered out in the early evening. Both sides were bloodied and tired. Although the Germans had fought their way across the canal it had come at a heavy cost in lives, and their formations were greatly disorganised. Similar confusion existed on the British side and it was impossible to speak of a coherent front line, with troops hopelessly intermingled amongst the winding streets.

It is misleading to assign victory or defeat to the Battle of Mons. The Germans had gained several bridgeheads across the canal, but the British could claim tactical success due to the damage inflicted on the attackers. Debate continues over the casualties of the battle. British losses were 1,600 men, with around half of these prisoners. German casualties were certainly higher but the destruction of the Prussian archives during a bombing raid in the Second World War makes it impossible to give exact numbers. German regimental histories published after the war suggest a total of 2,000 casualties, but evidence from Belgian civilians charged with collecting the dead gives a considerably higher figure. In his post-war memoirs, von Kluck admitted that German losses were 'heavy'. A German infantry officer gave a similar assessment, noting that after the battle 'we were compelled to admit that these English mercenaries – whom many of us before the war had looked down upon with disparagement and contempt – had in every case fought valiantly and tenaciously. This was sufficiently obvious from the heavy losses which our German troops had suffered here.'

Nevertheless, at the end of the fighting the soldiers of both sides believed that the battle would be renewed in the morning. In actual fact, the British would not see action at Mons again until November 1918. The Great Retreat was about to begin.

### The Retreat Begins

Smith-Dorrien recorded in his diary that he was 'quite happy' with the results of the Battle of Mons. He had always envisaged the engagement as a delaying action and felt it had achieved its objective. The BEF appeared to be in good shape. Losses in II Corps were light and Haig's I Corps had not been attacked at all during the battle.

However, the strategic situation had become extremely hazardous for the British Army. Interrogation of German prisoners revealed that the BEF had been fighting against the bulk of *First Army*. The incontrovertible information gained at Mons finally convinced Sir John French of the dangers which the army faced. Greatly outnumbered, with Lanrezac retreating on the right and the French territorials falling back on the left, the British were at risk of being encircled and annihilated. The only option was to retreat south and try to regain a position alongside Fifth Army. Late on 23 August GHQ issued orders for a withdrawal to take place under cover of darkness.

Whilst I Corps was able to disengage with relative ease, the same operation proved far harder for II Corps. It had spent the day engaged in fierce combat and in many places it was still in contact with German forces. Smith-Dorrien organised the withdrawal as best he could and the men began to slip away from the front line at around 4.00am. The disengagement was skilfully executed, prompting a German soldier to comment: 'Up to all the tricks of the trade from their experience of small wars, the English veterans brilliantly understood how to slip off at the last moment.' Realising that the British were withdrawing, von Kluck immediately launched a vigorous pursuit.

The Great Retreat was underway, and the harrowing trials of II Corps were about to begin.

# Chapter 4: Action at Audregnies

Smith-Dorrien's diary entry for 24 August noted: 'I saw Haig, and we settled on a course of action, as we both fully realised that we were in for a very heavy day's fighting and that the operation of withdrawal in the face of such numbers was a very serious and difficult one.' The assessment was correct. The rearguard fighting on 24 August was deemed too small scale to be granted the title of 'battle' by the post-war Battle Nomenclature Committee, but the total casualties suffered on this day were actually higher than those of the Battle of Mons.

The problem Smith-Dorrien faced was how to manoeuvre his two divisions away from the built up area of Mons without being attacked and overwhelmed on the march. 3rd Division, which had borne the brunt of the fighting on 23 August, slipped away first, fighting several skilful rearguard actions around Frameries and inflicting considerable damage on the pursuing Germans. Some German regiments were new to the area and attacked in the same massed formations that had cost their comrades dearly at Mons. Alf Tebbutt of the 1st Lincolns recalled: 'I just kept firing away at the mass of Germans in front me until my rifle was almost too hot to hold. At 400 yards you couldn't miss and I never thought to see so many dead and wounded men in such a small space.' A German officer wrote of a 'terrible fusillade...sweeping over bare fields whose hard sun-dried surface made every bullet a ricochet.' The post-war unit history for the *24th Infantry Regiment* admitted that the 'British defence was extraordinarily tough'.

However, although 3rd Division was able to withdraw relatively smoothly, 5th Division was not so fortunate. German infantry launched several ferocious attacks against the British rearguards, attempting to disrupt and slow the division so that flanking forces could encircle it. Infantry assaults were made from the direction of Mons and resulted in stiff fighting around the mining villages of Pâturages, Hornu and Wasmes. At the latter, the 2nd Duke of Wellington's Regiment failed to receive timely orders to withdraw and suffered heavy losses fighting its way clear.

But whilst attention was focused on the fighting to the north a far greater danger was approaching from the west. German forces had discovered the BEF's exposed left flank and sought to exploit the gap to get behind 5th Division and cut its line of retreat. Aware of the looming threat, 5th Division's commander, Major General Sir Charles Fergusson, detached the 1st Cheshires and 1st Norfolks to cover the vulnerable flank. The infantry were supported by the horsemen of 2nd Cavalry Brigade. It was vital that this rearguard held long enough for 5th Division to get away.

The seeds of the coming tragedy were sown in the rearguard's orders. Its commander, Lieutenant Colonel C.R. Ballard of the Norfolks, had initially been told to hold on at all costs. But this was later amended by written orders that gave him permission to withdraw when necessary. Ballard assumed that his co-commander, Lieutenant Colonel D.C. Boger of the Cheshires, had also received these instructions. But Boger had not been informed of the change and still believed that the rearguard was to fight to the last man.

The small force made its stand near the village of Audregnies at midday. There was no time to dig trenches. The infantry shook out into extended lines and took position along an old Roman road. Tom Lawrence of the 1st Norfolks recalled: 'We were on a little ridge, Cheshires on our left, 119th [RFA Battery] on our right, and a clear field of fire across cornfields to the northwest. Might have been back home in Norfolk!' Long grass and corn stooks provided a modicum of concealment but there was precious little cover. However, the position had good fields of fire that allowed the British to make maximum use of rifles and machine guns.

Within scant minutes of deployment the rearguard was under attack. The Germans advanced in overwhelming strength. *IV Corps* was swinging around to carry out the encirclement and its leading formations, *7th Division* and *8th Division*, were first into action. The assault was supported by a mass of artillery that hurled salvo after salvo at the rearguard's line. One British veteran recalled: 'The situation seemed pretty miserable as the fire was so heavy as to defy description.' The defenders had no way of responding and were forced to grit their teeth and endure the punishment.

With the rearguard blanketed by exploding shells, the German infantry advanced with confidence. But they were met by withering fire from rifles, machine guns and artillery. In an army that prided

44

itself on marksmanship, the Cheshires had a reputation as an outstanding 'shooting' battalion. Scurrilous pre-war rumour suggested that it was due to an unofficial reward system that offered bottles of beer in return for good scores on the range. These skills were used to devastating effect and the German advance was stopped dead in its tracks. The gunners of the Royal Artillery heaped further punishment on the attackers. The *Official History* described how the gunners 'opened upon them with shrapnel, bursting its shells low, with an accuracy which literally mowed down the advancing masses'.

But the sheer weight of the German attack was crushing. Repeated frontal assaults occupied British attention. Meanwhile, fresh German infantry began to slip around the flanks, seeking to encircle the rearguard. It was at this point that a controversial incident took place. 2nd Cavalry Brigade, concealed amongst trees and fighting dismounted, was protecting the left of the rearguard. However, enemy infantry were observed advancing with the intention of outflanking the Cheshires. The horsemen were commanded by Brigadier-General Beauvoir de Lisle, an aggressive leader who did not fit the stereotypical image of a cavalry officer. He had begun his career as an infantryman but became famous as a superb polo player – he popularised the polo shirt as an item of casual wear – and later joined the mounted branch. De Lisle observed the infantry advance and recognised that it posed a grave danger to the Cheshires. Yet he also saw that it offered a golden opportunity for a cold steel attack against an unsuspecting foe. He told his subordinates 'I'm going to charge the enemy' and launched the 9th Lancers and 4th Dragoon Guards into the fray.

Timing is crucial in war and mere minutes can mean the difference between victory and defeat. Unfortunately for de Lisle, in his eagerness to attack he mistimed his charge. The main body of German infantry had only just begun to emerge from a jumble of buildings when the attack began, and were able to turn and flee back to the safety of the brick walls when the cavalry emerged. Had de Lisle waited until the Germans were fully committed, he would have caught them on open ground with potentially devastating results.

It was not to be. Aside from a few unfortunate laggards, the German infantry was able to flee back to the buildings as the cavalry thundered towards them. Deprived of a clear target, the horsemen careened towards the German artillery line but ran into an agricultural barbed wire fence that prevented any further advance. Blinded by clouds of dust and flayed by fire from German artillery and machine guns, the cavalry lost all cohesion. One trooper remembered he 'could not see what we were charging either going or coming'. Another recalled that the mass of horsemen milled 'in disorder like a flock of sheep'. Lieutenant Grenfell Elliot of the Cheshires watched the attack break down, comparing it to the infamous charge of the Light Brigade in the Crimean War: 'It was Balaclava over again except that we never got the guns'. Bloodied and confused, the survivors swept across the battlefield and disappeared behind the right flank in complete disarray. The cavalry would play no further part in the battle.

The reckless charge removed the British flank guard and left the infantry dangerously isolated. The Germans redoubled their efforts to outflank the Cheshires and were soon pouring galling enfilade fire into the British position. With more and more German infantry battalions entering the battle, it was clear that the rearguard would be obliterated if it remained in place.

Around 2.30pm Ballard judged that it was time to go and ordered the Norfolks to fall back. Before he departed, Ballard sent withdrawal orders to the Cheshires, taking the precaution of dispatching three messengers by separate routes to ensure that the command was delivered safely. But luck did not favour the British. All the runners became casualties and the message never reached its intended recipient.

Without orders to the contrary the Cheshires stubbornly held their ground. It was a desperate contest against overwhelming numbers. By 4.00pm Boger had decided that the situation was critical and set out to find Ballard to discuss withdrawal. He headed to the right where he expected to find the Norfolks, only to discover the ground was occupied by enemy infantry who greeted him with a hail of bullets. Boger ran back to his battalion and began to give orders to retire, but was shot through the side and severely wounded before he had chance to organise a full withdrawal.

With other officers unaware of the dire situation, the fate of the Cheshires was sealed. Lieutenant Elliot recalled: 'The fire grew hotter & hotter, the sky was literally rent with shells & the shrapnel lashed the fields like hail.' The survivors battled on, surrounded and

47

under remorseless fire, until around 6.30pm. At this point, with ammunition exhausted and all prospect of escape gone, the surviving senior officer, Major Chetwynd-Stapylton, raised a white flag and gave orders to surrender. A large number of soldiers ignored the command and chose to fight to the bitter end. The battalion's casualties were dreadfully high. The Cheshires had mustered 959 officers and men at the beginning of the day; 788 were killed or captured at Audregnies.

But the sacrifice was not in vain. The rearguard had held off an extremely dangerous German flank attack and ensured the safety of 5th Division. The BEF had escaped, but further dangers lay ahead.

# Chapter 5: The BEF Splits

## Forced March

By 25 August it was clear that the Allied campaign was not going according to plan. The French had made no progress on the Franco-German border whilst both the BEF and Fifth Army had been driven from Belgium by superior German forces. Spearheads from German *First* and *Second Army* were in close pursuit and were driving into French territory. For the first time, French supreme commander Joseph Joffre began to perceive the shape of the Schlieffen Plan and recognise the grave danger it posed to France. He would spend the coming days racing against time to devise a counterstroke.

At BEF headquarters there were more immediate concerns. Von Kluck's attempt to encircle the BEF had been stopped at Audregnies, but *First Army* remained in pursuit. Sir John briefly considered retiring into the French fortress at Mauberge but wisely discounted the idea, recognising that it would only result in the army becoming trapped and besieged. Instead, he resolved that the BEF had to put distance between itself and its powerful opponent until a favourable opportunity arose to counterattack.

But the retreat was complicated by the terrain that lay ahead. The Forest of Mormal, a dense tract of woodland some 35 miles square, sat directly astride the BEF's route. Ideally the entire army would pass on a single side of the forest, but the conditions of the Great Retreat made this impossible. Moving both I and II Corps on one side of the woodland would overburden the road network and create huge traffic jams. This was an intolerable risk given that German pursuit was so close behind. The only option was to violate one of the cardinal rules of warfare and divide the army. Haig and I Corps would follow roads on the eastern side of the forest, whilst Smith-Dorrien and II Corps would travel to the west of the woodland. The two formations would reunite at the southern end. The decision was inadvisable but unavoidable.

The BEF was on the march at an early hour. Major Gordon-Lennox described the day in his diary: 'Off back again about 5am, a long and very hot march with continual gunning going on in our rear. They seem pushing devils these Germans.' Progress was often painfully slow due to traffic congestion. One officer recalled: 'a huge mass of British transport was struggling to pass through roads which were already seriously congested by a crowd of refugees. These, with every kind of vehicle, from six-horse farm wagons to perambulators, everywhere delayed the marching troops, and made it impossible for motor cars carrying Staff Officers to pass the columns.' An officer of the Royal Berkshires referred to the crowds of frightened civilians as a 'broken torrent of dusty misery'.

Stifling heat, long marches and lack of sleep were beginning to take a toll on the troops. A fully laden infantryman could expect to carry at least sixty pounds of equipment. This was a challenging burden at the best of times and one that proved unbearable for many soldiers on the retreat. As a result, troops cast aside extraneous pieces of kit such as great coats and shaving sets. A passing cavalryman commented: 'The infantry were extraordinary to look at; all had beards, they had discarded a lot of their equipment, and cut off sleeves above the elbow'. Conditions were especially hard on the reservists. Pale skin became painfully sunburnt and the newly issued boots resulted in dreadful blisters. Another horseman recalled: 'The men began to fall out a great deal on the road. The heat was very great. Many of the reservists were soft, and their feet found them out. Their rough clothes rubbed them.' Stragglers who could not keep up with the pace were usually captured by the pursuing Germans.

Yet despite these problems, the BEF marched hard on the 25 August. Most battalions covered at least 20 miles and several went considerably further. The army was aided by the wise decision of the Quartermaster General, Sir William Robertson, to dispense with normal methods of resupply in favour of placing large supply dumps of food at the roadside so that troops could take what they needed. The system was distinctly against War Office regulations but Robertson, a fiercely intelligent man and the only British soldier to ever rise from private to Field Marshal, recognised that desperate times required desperate measures. This system of resupply proved invaluable as the retreat dragged on.

### Night Attack at Landrecies

After a day of hard marching, I Corps set up its headquarters in the French village of Landrecies during the early evening. The formation had barely fired a shot in anger, but the demands of the retreat had left officers and men exhausted. I Corps' commander Douglas Haig was unwell. At the outset of the campaign he had been plagued by uncomfortable constipation. Captain John Charteris recalled that on the 24 August the senior medical officer had treated Haig's problem and 'dosed him with what must have been something designed for elephants, for the result was immediate and volcanic'. Haig was still suffering from the effects on 25 August and was forced to travel in a staff car rather than ride on horseback. Charteris commented that Haig was 'very chewed up and ghastly to look at'. Haig's ill-health would have a deleterious influence on coming events.

Landrecies was defended by 4th (Guards) Brigade. Aside from some brisk rearguard skirmishes, I Corps had seen little action on the 25 August and a number of officers had developed a casual assumption that the Germans had been left far behind. In fact, German infantry and cavalry were just a few miles from the village. Fortunately for the BEF the fog of war was equally blinding on the German side, and the advancing soldiers knew nothing about British dispositions. The *27th Infantry Regiment* had actually been ordered to head to Landrecies and rest there for the night, with their commander being assured the village was deserted as 'the English were in full retreat'. The scene was set for a confused encounter.

The 3rd Coldstream Guards had formed an outpost line at the northern edge of Landrecies, placing a single strand of barbed wire across the main road and covering the approaches with a machine gun. At around 7.30pm the defenders heard a column of troops approaching the village. The commander of the outpost, Captain

Charlie Monck, called out a challenge. The approaching soldiers responded by shining a torch in Monck's face and shouting 'Don't shoot!' in French. However, Monck, alerted by the sound of running feet in the darkness, bellowed for his men to open fire. It was too late. The Germans rushed the outpost with bayonets and kicked over the machine gun before it had the chance to get off more than a few rounds. Brutal hand to hand combat with bayonets and rifle butts raged along the line, but the arrival of Coldstream reinforcements turned the tide and the attackers were driven back into the shadows.

A sharp night action followed. The Germans poured a hail of bullets into the village and pressed forward through the surrounding fields. The Coldstream were soon reinforced by the 1st Grenadier Guards, who extended the line and beat back German attempts to infiltrate past the flanks of the British position. In the dim light the Guards displayed their lethal snap shooting skills, picking off enemy infantrymen as they attempted to dash between hedgerows. However, the situation deteriorated when a haystack near the British position caught fire and illuminated the defenders. Seizing the opportunity, a German field gun unlimbered just beyond sight of the front line and unleashed accurate shrapnel fire on the guardsmen. Seeking a response, the British manhandled a 4.5inch howitzer into a concealed firing position. The howitzer scored a direct hit with its third round, blasting apart the German gun and its crew. The sudden destruction of the field gun dissuaded further German attacks. Intermittent bursts of fire continued throughout the night but the Germans had received a bloody nose and were reluctant to press on, especially as they were unsure of exactly how many British troops opposed them. Both sides suffered around 130 casualties in the action.

However, the small engagement had a disproportionate influence on Douglas Haig. Haig had been alarmed by the sound of gunfire at the edge of the village and, according to Captain Charteris, had burst from his headquarters armed with a revolver declaring, 'If we are caught, by God, we sell our lives dearly'. His officers swiftly whisked him away in a staff car and thus Haig did not have a full grasp of events. Tired, ill and under considerable stress, Haig reacted with uncharacteristic panic and became convinced that the entirety of I Corps was in grave danger. He made a telephone call to GHQ in which he described the situation as 'very critical' and informed Sir John of his intention to continue retreating south, rather than turning south west and marching to the pre-planned rendezvous point with II Corps. The message unnerved GHQ, who gained the impression that I Corps had suffered a major defeat.

In the early hours Sir John French ordered II Corps to march to Haig's assistance. But the request was impossible, for Smith-Dorrien was about to fight the most important – and dangerous – battle of the entire campaign.

# Chapter 6: The Battle of Le Cateau

## The Crisis

The 25 August had been a torrid day for II Corps. German forces were in close proximity and were unaware that the British had separated to pass the Forest of Mormal. Instead, von Kluck believed that II Corps represented the entire BEF and he directed *First Army* to concentrate its full attention on destroying the retreating formation. The Germans scented blood. The roadsides were littered with abandoned BEF equipment and numerous British stragglers were captured. The expectation of victory drove the pursuers onwards through scorching heat and gruelling marches. The Germans had a key advantage in that any man who fell behind would eventually catch up. Infantry battalions marched forward in high spirits, convinced that the war would be over in a matter of days.

The British did not have this luxury. To fall behind on the retreat was to be lost. Officers and NCOs worked tirelessly to keep the men in line, but every arduous hour on the march made it harder to hold the battalions together. II Corps had fought fierce actions on the previous two days and desperately needed rest. Smith-Dorrien knew that this was impossible and drove his units onwards. Some of his battalions covered a blistering 30 miles on 25 August.

There was some good news for the British as they reached the town of Le Cateau. Reinforcements had arrived in the form of 4th Division, which had been transferred to France a few days earlier. These fresh troops stood guard as the exhausted veterans filed past. 4th Division's commander, Major General Sir Thomas Snow, remembered that he 'gleaned that the 3rd and 5th Divisions had been retreating and fighting for 36 hours, and that they had had about as much as any troops could stand.'

Smith-Dorrien had orders to continue the retreat the next morning. His corps was settling down to rest when disturbing news arrived at 11.00pm. Major General Edmund Allenby, commanding the Cavalry Division, reported that his horsemen were too scattered to guarantee protection on the march if II Corps moved on 26 August. The cavalry had spent the day fighting innumerable small rearguard actions and the division had lost cohesion as a result. The damage suffered by 2nd Cavalry Brigade at Audregnies worsened the situation.

Smith-Dorrien responded by calling his commanders together for a crisis meeting. By the time all were assembled it was almost 2.00am and the discussion was conducted by lamp light. The news was troubling. Smith-Dorrien asked if it would be possible for the infantry to retreat under cover of darkness, but learned that his exhausted men would not be able to move until 9.00am. To move off in daylight without a strong cavalry rearguard was very dangerous. The Germans were so close that they were certain to intercept II Corps on the march unless the British gained a substantial head start.

If the corps was caught in marching formation then it would undoubtedly be destroyed.

There was only one other option – turn and fight. The atmosphere was tense as Smith-Dorrien explained his plan to hold at Le Cateau, deal 'a stopping blow' to the pursuing Germans and then retire under the confusion caused by the action. He asked for the opinions of his fellow officers and, having received positive replies, stood straight and stated, 'Very well gentlemen, we will fight'. Allenby and Snow both agreed to place their formations under Smith-Dorrien's command even though he did not have formal authority over them.

The decision was a grave gamble. II Corps would face the German onslaught all but alone. Some French territorial cavalry covered the left flank whilst the right flank was entirely open. Smith-Dorrien hoped that I Corps would march to his support on the right, but Haig, panicked by events at Landrecies, refused to move. This meant that II Corps was in danger of being surrounded and destroyed by the superior numbers of *First Army*.

Yet there were some advantages to the position. The ground was open and offered good fields of fire for the defenders. Smith-Dorrien also judged that the coming battle would pose problems for the Germans. The defiant British stand would come as surprise after days of retreat. If the Germans chose to launch an immediate attack then they would have little time to reconnoitre the position, thus running the risk of being drawn into a frontal attack which Smith-Dorrien believed his men could hold off. However, more thorough preparations would take time, and every hour that the British could delay the Germans was precious.

At 5.00am a staff car arrived at GHQ carrying news of Smith-Dorrien's decision. Sir John French was awoken to receive the message and replied with a positive, albeit somewhat muddled, telegram which began, 'If you can hold your ground the situation appears likely to improve' and ended with the exhortation to 'make every endeavour' to continue the retirement. However, having considered the issue further, French changed his mind. At 6.45am GHQ contacted Smith-Dorrien and urged him to retreat immediately, but by then it was too late for the Battle of Le Cateau had already begun. Its outcome would determine the result of the Great Retreat.

## The Battle

The battlefield at Le Cateau was in striking contrast to that of Mons. One veteran remembered it as 'Salisbury Plain without the trees'. The ground was defined by gently rolling hills and open fields, intersected by a jumble of small roads and dotted with a handful of farming villages. The British line stretched approximately ten miles, with 4th Division on the left, 3rd Division in the centre and 5th Division on the right. The Cavalry Division was held in reserve. French territorial soldiers screened the western flank, but the eastern flank was dangerously exposed. Le Cateau itself marked the far right of the British position. Smith-Dorrien chose not to occupy the town for fear that any defenders would be surrounded and cut off. It was important to maintain mobility for when the time came to withdraw.

The infantry formed the backbone of the defence. The dog tired soldiers had had little time to prepare trenches. Some battalions created hasty 'scrapes', shallow individual positions in which a man could lie prone, but other regiments chose to fight in the open. Extra ammunition was distributed but some regiments had not had time to draw rations and went into battle hungry.

The footsloggers did not fight alone. In several places, particularly on the eastern flank, the gunners deployed their batteries in the front line. Although this went against the letter of pre-war regulations, it was very much in the spirit of the Royal Artillery, who lived by the credo 'the greater the difficulties of the infantry the closer should be the support of the artillery'. The decision was controversial. On one hand, the front line deployment allowed the gunners to pour ferocious close range fire onto the attacking German infantry. Conversely, the exposed positions made the guns a perfect target for German counter battery fire. The ultimate wisdom of the policy remains a topic of debate. What is certain is that it cost the Royal Artillery a heavy price in lives.

The German advance began in the pre-dawn light. As at Mons, the battle intensified as the day wore on and more enemy units arrived on the field; the British line was attacked by at least five German divisions with elements from several others joining the fighting as the hours ticked past. The assault troops were supported by a devastating mass of artillery, with the Germans able draw upon around 550 guns compared to approximately 228 possessed by the Royal Artillery. The German attack sought to carry out a double envelopment, simultaneously turning left and right flanks and cutting off all hope of retreat. As such, the attackers concentrated their assault against 4th Division and 5th Division. Although 3rd Division was also engaged, German efforts here were aimed at holding it in place until the flank attacks had succeeded.

The German attack began on the left. *II Cavalry Corps* rode onto the field supported by elite *jaeger* ('hunter') infantry transported in motor lorries. Their initial assault caught elements of 4th Division by surprise. The men of the 1st Kings Own were awaiting breakfast rations and the battalion was in close column formation when it was suddenly flayed by a terrible barrage of German machine gun fire, suffering four hundred casualties in less than two minutes. The 1st Royal Warwickshire's launched a hurried counterattack to cover the withdrawal of the survivors. Lieutenant Bernard Montgomery – who would ultimately rise to command British 8th Army at the Battle of El Alamein in 1942 – took part in the Warwicks' charge. He remembered: 'there was no reconnaissance, no plan, no covering fire...waving my sword I ran forward in front of my platoon, but unfortunately I had only gone six paces when I tripped over my scabbard, the sword fell away from my hand...and I fell flat on my face on very hard ground.' In fact, his stumble was fortunate, for most of the attackers were killed or wounded in the assault.

Yet from this low point the battle on the left began to incline in the favour of the British. Unable to charge home on horseback, *II Cavalry Corps* was drawn into a bitter dismounted engagement. Although the supporting *jaegers* were formidable infantry, the

German cavalry were not as well trained as their BEF counterparts and were inexperienced in dismounted fighting. Furthermore, the horsemen carried carbines that were distinctly inferior to the British Lee-Enfields. In the fierce battle that followed, the Germans lost sight of their primary objective – to turn the British flank – and instead focused on capturing small villages and ridges that were of no great strategic value. 4th Division fought stubbornly, inflicting heavy losses on the attackers but giving ground when necessary. By mid-afternoon the German attack had been brought to a bloody halt. Future official historian James Edmonds was serving as a staff officer for 4th Division at the time; he recalled that when he went forward at dusk to deliver withdrawal orders, the battlefield was so uncannily silent that he thought for a moment that all the combatants had been killed. In reality the Germans had been fought to a standstill and had no desire to press the action any further. The attack had petered out and 4th Division was able to slip away without interference.

However, the situation on the right flank was very different. The main weight of the German attack fell on this position. Around dawn a powerful concentration of enemy artillery had unlimbered on a ridge approximately 3800 yards from the British line. From here they had a perfect view of 5th Division's line and were able to rain a devastating storm of fire onto the defenders. The deadly consequences of the Royal Artillery's forward deployment were now revealed. The Germans had no need to split their fire between artillery and infantry. Instead, they could concentrate every shot against the front line and be virtually certain that they would hit something.

For the British, the result was a gunner's nightmare. Outnumbered and outgunned, the Royal Artillery could offer little in the way of return fire. The gallant batteries were pounded remorselessly, losing guns, limbers, horses and crewmen to the constant barrage. John Lucy, fighting with 3rd Division, remembered the effects: 'blinding flashes of concentrated explosions licked all about our single gallant field battery, which had been quickly marked down by the enemy, and which gradually slackened fire until it was ultimately smashed into silence.' Alongside them the infantry suffered equally. Their hastily dug foxholes offered little protection from the thunderous high explosive shells and screaming hail of shrapnel that swept the British line. Stunned by concussive blasts, choked by cordite fumes and showered by a rain of lead, the defenders could only grit their teeth and await their chance to strike back. As one officer noted with quiet understatement, 'the moral effect of lying still without being able to fire a shot in reply is very hard on even the strongest nerves.'

The Germans were patient. The Battle of Mons had taught them the cost of premature attacks and now they waited for the gunners to finish their deadly work. Machine gun teams pressed forward to add their metronomic fire to the bombardment. One enterprising crew managed to carry their gun to the top of Le Cateau's church tower, where it was able to pour harrowing enfilade fire into the defenders. A British soldier remembered that the bullets came so thick and fast that they shredded long grass 'just as if by a mowing machine.'

At 10.00am, after almost four hours of shelling, German infantry began to advance in earnest. The first wave of attackers rushed forward in extended skirmish order, but behind them came heavy assault lines with soldiers separated by little more than a yard per man. It was a perfect target for the surviving British gunners and they wasted no time in seizing the opportunity. British shrapnel tore through the massed ranks, with one Royal Artillery officer recalling the enemy formation was 'like a target at practice camp...each gathering line of Germans was laid low.' The attackers who survived this barrage stumbled forward and were met by concentrated rifle and machine gun fire. A German veteran recalled: 'Our men attacked with the utmost determination, but again and again they were driven back by those incomparable soldiers. Regardless of loss, the English artillery came forward to protect their infantrymen and in full view of our own guns kept up a devastating fire.'

But the Germans continued to attack. Renewed assaults were launched from the north. Groups of infantry managed to reach positions amongst trees and in dead ground, which then served as a rallying point for reinforcements. Savage fire fights followed as the Germans tried to advance from these lodgements and the British fought to hold them back. Meanwhile the enemy artillery redoubled its efforts to crush the defenders. German spotter aircraft circled overhead with impunity, dropping silver streamers to indicate priority targets. Although the British line held, the relentless hammer of shell fire was slowly crushing 5th Division to death.

63

The crisis point came in the early afternoon. As the battle raged at the front, German troops started to slip around the eastern end of Le Cateau and probe along 5th Division's exposed right flank. More and more enfilade fire began to come from this direction. Worse still, there was a grave risk that the enemy would realise the extent of the gap and use it to cut off the British retreat. Smith-Dorrien was conscious of the danger and knew that it was time to withdraw. Orders were given for the retirement to progress right to left, with 5th Division getting away first.

The instructions arrived not a moment too soon. Even tough, professional soldiers had a limit to their endurance. 5th Division had taken a frightful pounding. Commander Charles Fergusson noted that it was beginning to 'dribble away' as wounded and broken men drifted back from the front line. In some parts of the British line there was a dangerous sense of panic. John Lucy remembered seeing a group of soldiers fleeing in disorder until they were calmed by a staff officer, 'his face hot with the shame of it' shouting at them 'For God's sake men, be British soldiers.'

The withdrawal was no easy matter. This was especially true for the Royal Artillery. Smashed limbers and heavy casualties amongst men and horses made moving the guns a herculean trial. German infantry was now so close to the British line that they could shoot down approaching horse teams. Heroic efforts were made to save the guns, with many brave volunteers falling to enemy fire. 2nd Lieutenant Clarrie Hodgson recalled an incident at 122nd Battery: 'The order came down – *Save the guns*! And the gun teams came dashing down, over the hill, right through the middle of this carnage. And the Hun opened up on them – artillery, machine-guns, everything...It was *absolute slaughter*! Men and horses were just blown to pieces.' Only one of the guns from the battery was brought away safely. In total the British lost 38 artillery pieces at the battle, some destroyed by direct hits, but many abandoned on the field.

Yet overall the withdrawal of the British divisions proceeded reasonably, perhaps remarkably, well. There were certainly problems. Orders to retire failed to reach some front line units. On the right, the 2nd Suffolks had been told that the battle was a fight to the finish and that there would be no retreat. The order was never rescinded and the battalion fought on until it was finally overrun and destroyed. In the centre the 1st Gordon Highlanders did not receive news of the retirement and became isolated. They doggedly held their ground until darkness and then tried to fight their way back towards the rest of II Corps, but became trapped behind German lines and were forced to surrender at 3.00am.

Of those that did retreat, many battalions were jumbled up with one another and there were isolated incidents of panic. In some cases small groups had become separated from the main body of the army. The young Bernard Montgomery was amongst one of these latter groups and endured a harrowing time as he and his comrades zig-zagged across the countryside, dodging enemy cavalry patrols, until they finally rejoined their battalion. But as a whole II Corps was able to retire safely. Smith-Dorrien watched his men go and thought they were 'a wonderful sight: men smoking their pipes, apparently quite unconcerned, and walking steadily down the road – no formation of any sort, and men of all units mixed up together. I likened it to a crowd coming away from a race meeting.'

The key reason for the successful withdrawal was the complete absence of German pursuit. Smith-Dorrien's 'stopping blow' had achieved its objective. *First Army* had driven the British back but the effort had left the Germans bloodied and exhausted. A handful of German patrols moved forward at dusk, but they withdrew when fired upon and showed no inclination to renew the fighting against the defiant British rearguards. Von Kluck contented himself by reporting, erroneously, that he had fought and destroyed the entire BEF, 'six divisions, a cavalry division and several French Territorial divisions.' This was wrong. Von Kluck claimed in his post-war memoirs that he had hoped for another chance to fight the British on 27 August. His actions do not support this theory, and regardless, the opportunity had slipped away forever. *First Army* spent the night camped on the battlefield licking its wounds. German cavalry headed west on the assumption that the British would retreat towards Calais. Meanwhile, II Corps was marching south at a brisk pace, with every hour taking it further from von Kluck's grasp.

The Battle of Le Cateau was a vital victory for the BEF, but it came at a high cost in blood. Official British casualties were 7,812 men killed, wounded or missing. As previously noted, it is impossible to give exact losses for *First Army* due to the destruction of archival paperwork. However, a detailed study produced by the

British War Department in 1933, when the original documents were still available, listed German losses as 8,970 killed and wounded.

Historian John Terraine considered the stand at Le Cateau 'the most brilliant exploit of the BEF on the retreat.' Cavalryman Colonel John Vaughan believed the victory 'made the rest of our retreat possible and easy.' He was only half correct. Despite Smith-Dorrien's battlefield triumph, the coming days would be anything but easy.

# Chapter 7: Surrender and Sacrifice

## Surrender at St. Quentin

The night of 26/27 August was a trial of endurance for the men of II Corps. They had fought all day and now marched all night. John Lucy remembered: 'Our minds and bodies shrieked for sleep...Men slept while they marched, and they dreamed as they walked...One sergeant kept up a long dirge for hours on end about his lost pack, yet he was still wearing it'. Captain Tudor St. John recalled being 'nearly asleep all the time we were marching' and as a result he 'imagined all sorts of weird sights.'

Dawn brought no relief. The day was stiflingly hot and the sunlight revealed, according to St. John 'signs of hurried retreat, overturned motor vehicles, and wagons and dead horses' although 'nowhere among this was to be seen the rifles or ammunition carried by the exhausted infantry'. Officers worked tirelessly to maintain unit cohesion. St. John was disgusted by the sight of broken men sitting dejectedly at the roadside and resolved: 'This was not to happen in the ranks of the FIFTH...all the time [I was] urging persuading and even kicking men on.' Despite exhaustion, heat and sleeplessness, II Corps kept up the pace.

However, the day was marred by a notorious incident at the town of St. Quentin. British troops were evacuating the area, either on foot, in trains, or on wagons. Frederick Coleman, an American civilian who had volunteered as a staff car chauffeur remembered seeing 'rare scenes and strange sights' as overworked staff officers tried to impose some form of order on the confusion.

The 1st Royal Warwickshires and 2nd Royal Dublin Fusiliers had arrived at the town in the afternoon. It was initially believed that trains would take the battalions onwards. Whilst waiting for the locomotives, the shattered men seized the opportunity to rest. One cavalryman remembered: 'The whole square was thronged with British infantrymen... Scores had gone to sleep sitting on the pavement, their backs against the fronts of the shops. Many exhausted men lay at full length on the pavement.'

But whilst the soldiers rested, a crisis had overtaken their commanding officers, Lieutenant Colonel J.F. Elkington of the Royal Warwickshires and Lieutenant Colonel A.E. Mainwaring of the Dublin Fusiliers. They were negotiating with the mayor of the town over the provision of trains when a frightened civilian burst in carrying a report that claimed the town was surrounded by Germans. According to Mainwaring this caused the mayor to fall into despair, insisting that all was lost and that the enemy would destroy the town and its inhabitants. Deciding that capitulation was the only option, the mayor harangued Elkington and Mainwaring, insisting that they sign a document of 'unconditional surrender' that would hand over their battalions to the Germans without a fight. The two officers were exhausted, confused and uncertain that their men were capable of marching any further. To their shame, they signed the mayor's document and allowed the French authorities to disarm a number of their soldiers preparatory to marching into German captivity.

But there was a twist to the tale. In the late afternoon, the dusty horsemen of the 4th Dragoon Guards clattered into the town. They were operating as part of the rearguard and commanded by Major Tom Bridges. The major and his men had taken part in the charge at Audregnies on the 24 August. Bridges' horse had been shot from under him in the attack and he had then been trampled by the rest of the squadron, and, to add further injury, the machine gun section. Bruised and concussed, he had barely escaped from the debacle, ultimately being spirited away by an officer driving a blue and silver Rolls Royce!

On arrival at St. Quentin, Bridges reported that the Germans were still some distance away and that there was time for the battalions to get clear. However, the sullen infantry 'refused to march on the grounds that they had already surrendered and would only come away if a train was sent to take them.' Bridges, although backed by 'some hefty henchmen, farriers and the like', found that the men would not respond to appeals or threats. Quick thinking was required. Bridges' account explains what happened next: 'There was a toy-shop handy which provided my trumpeter and myself with a tin whistle and drum and we marched round and round the fountain where the men were lying like the dead playing *The British Grenadier* and *Tipperary* and beating the drum like mad. They sat up and began to laugh and even cheer. I stopped playing and made them

70

a short exhortation and told them I was going to take them back to their regiments. They began to stand up and fall in.'

Bridges' inventive method worked. Screened by the 4th Dragoon Guards, the rallied battalions marched away to safety. However, Elkington and Mainwaring faced court martial for their actions. In September 1914, both were found guilty and were cashiered from the army. Mainwaring privately published a book defending his conduct before fading into obscurity. Conversely, Elkington sought redemption. He enlisted anonymously in the French Foreign Legion and fought in several ferocious battles before being gravely wounded in September 1915. His courage was rewarded with the *Médaille Militaire* and the *Croix de Guerre avec Palme*. When his actions came to light, the British Army reinstated his rank of lieutenant colonel and awarded him the Distinguished Service Order. He died in 1944 with his honour restored.

Fortunately for the BEF, the incident at St. Quentin was decidedly atypical. Although II Corps' retreat on 27 August was a gruelling experience, there were no comparable breakdowns of discipline. The formation was still seriously disorganised but order was slowly being restored. Smith-Dorrien and his staff worked tirelessly to put the corps back into fighting shape and the subsequent days of the retreat, although still exhausting for those doing the marching, would proceed without undue incident.

Unfortunately, GHQ saw things differently. Sir John had plunged into a chasm of despair. French defeats and the seemingly unstoppable German advance had shaken his nerve. The Battle of Le

71

Cateau tipped him over the edge. French was furious that Smith-Dorrien had chosen to fight rather than retreat, and was convinced that II Corps had been virtually destroyed. At the very moment that the fortunes of the BEF were beginning to turn, the commander of the army was mired in a mental defeat. French began to consider withdrawing the BEF from battle entirely, a line of thought that would lead to a spectacular confrontation at the end of the month.

## Sacrifice at Étreux

The events surrounding II Corps understandably occupied GHQ's attention. However, to the east, I Corps was experiencing problems of its own. Haig's health was improving but his nerves were still shaken. He had declined Smith-Dorrien's request for assistance at Le Cateau and spent the 26 August in a state of inaction. The battle was clearly audible from I Corps' position and there were murmurings that the formation should follow army tradition and march to the sound of the guns. Haig refused to move, contenting himself with a half-hearted offer of support that was only issued at 8.30pm, long after the fighting had finished. The reasons behind this decision are a subject of debate amongst historians, but the evidence lends itself to an uncharitable interpretation.

Haig intended to continue I Corps' retreat on 27 August. His primary concern was the problem of road congestion. French soldiers from Fifth Army were using the same road network as the British, resulting in traffic jams and frayed tempers. Haig took an uncompromising attitude, insisting his men had priority and threatening to 'fight' the French for the route. Ultimately, the British

72

commander got his way. But whilst Haig's eyes were focused on the practicalities of the retreat, a disaster was about to engulf his rearguard.

Up to this point I Corps had not been seriously troubled by enemy pursuit. However, a strong force of German infantry and cavalry from *Second Army*, originally ordered to pursue Lanrezac's French troops, had stumbled across the British. These pursuers were fresh and attacked with vigour.

I Corps' rearguard was provided by 1st (Guards) Brigade, under the command of the highly rated Brigadier General Ivor Maxse. His orders were to cover I Corps until it had cleared the town of Étreux, and then fall back and join the main body. Timing was critical. It was essential that the defenders did not withdraw too soon and allow the Germans to shell the retreating columns.

The 2nd Munster Fusiliers took position at the centre of the rearguard. Army legend suggested that Guards brigades always included a tough Irish battalion to 'stiffen' the fighting power of the ceremonially inclined guardsmen. The Munsters certainly fitted the bill. On the day of the battle they were commanded by Major Paul Charrier, a quirky character who wore a pith helmet rather than a regulation cap and who was frequently seen in tropical shorts. Charrier's eccentricities concealed a sharp mind and a professional attitude. He was an expert in French and German military methods. Convinced that a major European conflict was inevitable, he had trained his men to a peak of efficiency.

73

The day dawned with grey skies and breathless humidity. At around 10.30am the rearguard was attacked by a mixed German force of cavalry, infantry and artillery. The engagement was fought across agricultural fields that were crisscrossed with drainage ditches and thick hedgerows. These covered approaches complicated the action considerably. The weather provided a further problem, for a violent thunderstorm broke over the area in the latter part of the morning. Visibility plummeted and the Germans seized the opportunity to close in on the defenders.

Yet despite these difficulties the rearguard had the better of the fighting. German attacks were initially uncoordinated and the British exploited the terrain to carry out deadly ambushes. A German post-war account remembered: 'Everywhere thick hedges! We are always getting fired on, we can't tell from where!' By midday the defenders had fulfilled their task and I Corps was clear of Étreux. Maxse despatched messengers ordering the rearguard to retire 'at once'. Unfortunately, the cyclist detailed to carry the instructions to the Munsters became lost in the maze of rain slicked fields and could not find Charrier.

At 1.15pm a message from Charrier arrived at brigade headquarters: 'Am holding on to position north of Femsy village, being attacked by a force of all arms. Getting on well. The Germans are driving cattle in front of them up to us for cover. We are killing plenty of them.' A final message arrived at 1.50pm noting that the Munsters had taken prisoners from *15th Regiment*. Sadly, the messengers who delivered the news were unable to find their way back to the battalion with fresh orders. This combination of the friction of war and the limitations of 1914 communications would result in tragedy.

Seeing that the Munsters remained heavily engaged, the 1st Coldstream Guards and 1st Black Watch delayed their own retirement until 4pm, holding their positions and keeping the route open for the Irish battalion to retire. Maxse later noted: 'they compromised the safety of themselves and the whole force by their prolonged delay, but I cannot for one moment blame either of them'. But it was all for nought. Without orders to withdraw the Munsters refused to give ground, only falling back when compelled to do so by enemy action. The very effectiveness of their defence sealed their fate.

By 5.00pm the supporting battalions had been forced to withdraw. The Munsters were alone except for some guns of the Royal Artillery. With enemy forces closing in, Charrier conducted a fighting retreat back to Étreux, arriving at around 6.00pm. But by now the Germans controlled the area. The road to the south was blocked and the battalion was surrounded. Attempts to fight their way out of the village proved fruitless. Charrier was wounded several times before he was finally killed leading a charge against German infantry. Outnumbered 6 to 1 and under fire from all sides, the Munsters fought to the bitter end. The last survivors were overwhelmed around 9.15pm.

The next day the Munsters were able to muster just 5 officers and 196 men. Maxse was blamed for the loss and was removed from his post in September. He would not find redemption until the Battle of the Somme in 1916. However, the Munster's stand had delayed the German advance. James Edmonds concluded after the war: 'Beyond question, they had arrested the enemy's pursuit in this quarter for fully six hours, so that their sacrifice was not in vain.' The stand ensured that the main body of I Corps would not be troubled by German pursuit for several days.

# Chapter 8: Cavalry Action

## Breathing Space

After the fierce fighting of the 26 and 27 the BEF finally found room to breathe on the 28 August. I Corps and II Corps were still separated by a gap of some 15 miles, but the slackening of German pursuit following the stopping blow at Le Cateau meant that the retreat had become a test of endurance rather than a life or death struggle.

Nevertheless, the physical and mental challenges were still enormous. Several officers, including James Edmonds, suffered nervous breakdowns and there was at least one case of suicide. Furthermore, Sir John French and his senior staff were still gripped by a sense of panic. On 27 August, GHQ issued a notorious order to II Corps ordering the formation to abandon all excess equipment, load up stragglers on wagons, and 'hustle along'. The order was issued directly to the divisions and bypassed Smith-Dorrien's headquarters. 3rd Division and 5th Division simply ignored the command, but 4th Division put it into practice. This was unfortunate: being ordered to abandon equipment created alarm amongst the men, who began to believe that the retreat was about to turn into a rout. Morale dropped and officers of the division complained that discipline declined. Undoubtedly the order made 4th Division's campaign unnecessarily difficult.

Smith-Dorrien only heard of the command after 4th Division had implemented it. Realising that his own authority had been bypassed, he flew into a rage and immediately drove to GHQ, where he met Sir John French and 'spoke with some heat'. Given Smith-Dorrien's infamous temper, the tone of the meeting can be well imagined.

The tragedy was that the order was entirely unnecessary. II Corps was disordered as a result of the Battle of Le Cateau, but it was steadily recovering and far from a broken formation. Curiously, even Sir John admitted as much after inspecting the retreating units on 28 August. He wrote in his diary: 'I had a most agreeable surprise. I met the men and talked to them as they were lying around resting. ½ million of these would walk over Europe. The 5. Division has quite recovered and its units are reorganized and in perfect trim, but with terrible gaps in the ranks.' Smith-Dorrien agreed with the assessment, commenting in his diary that his men: 'could not understand why we were retiring, for they considered they had given as good as they got every time they had met the Germans, and were anxious to go at them again.'

By 29 August German pursuit had been left so far behind that the BEF was allowed to take a much needed rest day. The formation owed these peaceful hours to the British cavalry, who were engaged in running rearguard actions to the north.

### Cavalry Action

Popular imagination has developed a warped view of cavalry in the First World War, typically seeing it as a hopelessly outdated irrelevance. This is misleading. In 1914 the mounted branch was an essential component of all major armies. Indeed, the success of the British cavalry in holding back German pursuit on the Great Retreat was vital to the survival of the BEF as a whole.

As previously discussed, British cavalry was trained to an extremely high standard. Its marksmanship was considered the equal of the infantry whilst its prowess in mounted combat was without question. Furthermore, British cavalry were well equipped with machine guns and artillery. The horsemen had need of all these assets, for they were gravely outnumbered by their German opposites. The single British cavalry division was, on paper, opposed by five German cavalry divisions. Fortunately, the Germans dispersed their mounted strength and diminished their overwhelming numerical advantage. Nevertheless, in the majority of cavalry engagements the British found themselves outnumbered.

The cavalry actions of the Great Retreat rarely featured the glamorous charges immortalised by battlefield artists. Instead, they were a series of rearguard engagements that typically involved ambush tactics and swift withdrawals. The British cavalry was well trained in 'protective reconnaissance' – the duty of blinding the enemy's scouting forces – but this was dangerous and difficult work. Screening parties would often occupy isolated forward positions and could not count on receiving support if things went wrong. Timing was crucial. If an ambush was triggered too early the Germans would avoid its effects and counterattack, but if it was left too late then the enemy would be so close that the defenders would be unable to withdraw to safety.

The aim of any rearguard action was to cause maximum delay to the pursuers. The British cavalry proved themselves adept at this duty. Equipped with Lee-Enfield rifles that outranged the German cavalry carbine, the British were able to open fire at long range and scatter approaching enemy patrols. The Germans would then be forced to call up their supporting *jaeger* infantry to clear the British position, but this would take time and imposed critical delays. Furthermore, once the Germans were ready to attack, the British cavalry would slip away to another defensive position and the process would begin once more.

The Great Retreat was marked by almost continuous cavalry rearguard action. The majority of the engagements were so small that they barely receive a mention in the unit War Diaries, but they had a cumulative effect of seriously disrupting German pursuit. A German infantry captain left an evocative description of facing British rearguards:

'...it must be admitted that in making use of cover and in offering a stubborn defence the English performed wonders. When we advanced against their first position we were received with rifle-fire, then they vanished, only to pop up in a second position. They were dismounted cavalrymen whose horses were hidden farther back, and, after decoying us to their third line, they mounted and fled. Between two of their trenches we found the dead horses of a patrol of Uhlans which they had apparently ambushed.'

Cavalryman John Darling commented after the war that British patrols 'by their bold action must have caused the enemy delay and inconvenience out of all proportion to their numerical strength.'

### Cold Steel at Cerizy

One of the most striking – and important – rearguard actions of the Great Retreat took place on 28 August near the village of Cerizy. Although the bulk of *First Army* had lost touch with the BEF after the Battle of Le Cateau, German cavalry continued the pursuit. On 28 August, elements of *Guards Cavalry Division* began to advance into the fifteen mile gap that lay between I Corps and II Corps. If this movement was allowed to continue unchecked then there was a grave danger that the horsemen would be able to attack one of the British formations in the flank, or even get behind it and block its retreat.

5th Cavalry Brigade was detailed to stop the German advance. The British horsemen reached the small village of Cerizy at about 10.30am. The hamlet was situated in picturesque French countryside. The ground was made up of gently rolling valleys, small copses of trees and agricultural fields. The Royal Scots Greys took a forward defensive position, deploying machine guns and dismounted troopers in patches of woodland. The 20th Hussars and 12th Lancers were placed in reserve a little further back. These men took advantage of the halt to rest weary horses and catch up on much needed sleep.

The tranquillity was shattered in the early afternoon. Gunfire erupted to the north as the advancing Germans ran into the Scots Greys. A sharp action followed. The weight of the German attack caused the Greys to give ground, but the superior marksmanship of the British troopers prevented the enemy making much progress. Determined to break through the rearguard, the Germans sought to turn the British flank by deploying reinforcements from the *2nd Guard Dragoons*. However, the attackers were soon spotted and engaged by rifles, machine guns and artillery. The Germans were forced to dismount and take cover in a field, but in the process their horses were panicked by British shell fire and stampeded away to the north. The German horsemen were thus stripped of their mobility and left in a very dangerous position. Nevertheless, they continued the fight.

But the British were about to make a flanking move of their own. Whilst the Scots Greys held the enemy's attention, the 12th Lancers mounted up and moved forward to attack the German left flank. The original plan had called for the cavalry to seize a dismounted position and pour enfilade fire upon the *2nd Guard Dragoons*, but the 12th Lancers soon discovered that the terrain favoured a mounted charge. The Germans were atop a small plateau, but it was possible to use dead ground to approach the position undetected and then launch an all-out charge at the last possible moment. If executed correctly, the surprise would be complete and the results would be decisive.

Cavalry officers dreamed of such opportunities, but the situation demanded precise timing. To rush the attack risked a debacle, as had occurred at Audregnies on the 24 August. Yet to take too long would give the Germans time to realise the danger and slip away. The tension was incredible, but the commander of the 12th Lancers, Lieutenant-Colonel Frank Wormald, held his nerve. He ordered his men to advance at walking pace so as not to tire the horses. The sound of gunfire ahead revealed the approximate position of the enemy. As the lancers approached the lip of the plateau Wormald bellowed 'gallop!' and soon after 'charge!'. The squadron trumpeter blasted out the bugle call: 'Let 'em go, at 'em boys, now for a charge!' Seconds later a thundering mass of horsemen burst over the plateau edge with lances at the ready.

The dismounted Germans were stunned. The 12th Lancers' regimental history recorded: 'The surprise was complete and terrible. As the lance-points and fluttering pennons bore down upon them a few Germans, shaken by the sight, cowered along the roots amongst which they were lying, but most rose to fight it out.' The contemporary war diary confirmed the assessment, noting that the *Guard Dragoons* 'fought exceedingly gallantly.'

But courage counted for little against the oncoming torrent. Wormald rode at the head of his men and impaled one dragoon 'so thoroughly that his sword buckled and remained firmly embedded in the German's body'. Another officer claimed to have cut down five of the enemy, noting that his sword 'went in and out of the Germans like a pat of butter.' The lancers crashed through the German line, then wheeled about and charged again. In total the 12th Lancers charged through the position three times. It was a bloody business. It is a brutal fact of war that it is almost impossible to surrender to a charging cavalryman; the overwhelming adrenaline of the charge turns even highly trained soldiers into the savage warriors of an earlier age. At the end of the third and final charge, only four Germans were left unwounded. The chaplain of *Guard Cavalry Division* noted that amongst the casualties there 'were men with six or seven lance wounds, and several bullet wounds.'

By the end of the action the *2nd Guard Dragoons* had been effectively destroyed and their supporting forces had been driven away. The British cavalry was understandably proud of the action at Cerizy (the 12th Lancers preferred to call it Moy) although German authors felt the scale of the victory had been exaggerated. The action was comparatively small but its effects were significant. The German attempt to exploit the gap between I Corps and II Corps had been decisively repulsed. The victory here permitted the BEF to take a rest day on 29 August and ensured that there would be no significant threat to the army for several days.

# Chapter 9: The Tide Turns

## The Swing of the Pendulum

The four days from the Battle of Mons to the action at Étreux had been desperately hard on the BEF. The French, especially Lanrezac's Fifth Army, had endured similar trials. Meanwhile, the German invasion continued to rumble through northern France.

However, the tide was beginning to turn. *First Army* had suffered heavy losses in the bruising encounters with the British Expeditionary Force. Although von Kluck clung to the hope that the BEF had been destroyed at Le Cateau, he had lost touch with his quarry and was now groping forwards blindly. British cavalry screens beat off German reconnaissance attempts and left the German commander in an intelligence vacuum. Marching into the unknown, *First Army's* advance had swung further to the west than originally intended. A dangerous gap was beginning to open between von Kluck's force and German *Second Army* to the east.

The seeds of German defeat were to be found in this loss of cohesion. *Second Army* was forced to drift to the west to try and close the gap. This movement exposed its flank to a French counterattack. On 29 August, Joffre gave Lanrezac a direct order to strike *Second Army*, resulting in a local yet important French victory at the Battle of Guise. Although Lanrezac's men were unable to hold their ground and resumed the retreat the next day, von Bülow was greatly alarmed by the developments and appealed to von Kluck for support. Von Kluck responded by turning his army from a south westerly course to a south easterly one which would bring him closer to *Second Army*. But this meant that the German advance would no longer sweep around Paris, as the original Schlieffen Plan had intended, but would instead pass to the east of the city. This seemingly minor change would have decisive consequences. It gave Joffre the time and space to assemble a new force, Sixth Army, based at Paris. This formation would play a decisive role at the Battle of the Marne in early September.

However, for several crucial days there was some doubt whether the BEF would remain in the field long enough to take part in this great engagement.

## The Decision

The last days of August were comparatively quiet for the BEF. The retreat continued and the tired infantry suffered under the baking sun, but the actual combat of this period was the preserve of the cavalry rearguards. The British cavalry skilfully parried away German probes and ensured that I Corps and II Corps were not troubled by the enemy.

Yet the relative calm could not disguise the fact that the BEF had been retreating for a full week since its engagement at Mons. Officers and men were frustrated at this development. This was particularly true in I Corps, which had barely fired a shot in anger. But the army marched on, grumbling and footsore, but unbroken.

Unfortunately, the stoicism of the men stood in contrast to the sense of despair that prevailed at GHQ. It is perhaps too easy to criticise Sir John French for his unpredictable mood swings. It is important to remember the circumstances which he faced. His army was on the retreat, his men were tired and battle-worn, and his French allies appeared to be in disarray. The latter point weighed particularly heavily on Sir John. He confessed: 'My confidence in the ability of the leaders of the French Army to carry this campaign to a successful conclusion is fast waning.' If France were to be defeated, then it was important that the BEF lived to fight another day. Sir John was deeply conscious that his force represented Britain's *only* combat ready army. If the BEF was destroyed then it could not be replaced. In such circumstances Sir John can perhaps be forgiven for losing his nerve, although it must be noted that Haig and Smith-Dorrien were both considerably more resolute.

However, what French failed to understand was that the campaign was a life and death struggle. The fate of France hung in the balance. By this stage British commitment was not optional – it was essential. Sir John could not simply withdraw the BEF and then return as and when he chose: he might find there was nothing but a victorious German army left to greet his return.

On 30 August Sir John bluntly informed Joffre that the BEF was unable to undertake combat operations 'for at least 10 days' and that he intended to withdraw the force behind the lines to recuperate. The decision caused alarm in London. Secretary of State for War Lord Kitchener was appalled by the news. He telegraphed French, asking:

'What will be the effect of this course upon your relations with the French Army and on the general military situation?', going on to express concern that any sudden withdrawal might allow the Germans to crush France before turning against Russia. Sir John was defiant, dismissing the abilities of the French military and offering contradictory statements that confirmed his intention to retreat, but simultaneously suggested his desire to attack! This garbled message was too much for Kitchener, who announced his intention to visit French in person on 1 September.

A tense meeting followed. Kitchener arrived in his Field Marshal's uniform and, according to French, 'from the outset his conversation assumed the air of a Commander-in-Chief'. Sir John was a prickly character at the best of times and was immediately offended by this perceived slight to his own authority. What was actually said at the meeting is unclear. Kitchener left no account of it and Sir John's prejudiced reminiscences are considered unreliable. However, the discussion had an important outcome. Sir John's plan to remove the BEF from the line was overruled, and although the retreat continued for the time being, it was agreed that it was only a temporary measure prior to a general Allied counterattack. The British would not withdraw from the fighting. The BEF would hold its place in the line and support their allies as best as it could.

It was a fateful decision that ensured the British Army would play a role at the decisive Battle of the Marne. But there were still dangers to be faced on the retreat.

# Chapter 10: Final Clashes

The final engagements of the Great Retreat were accidental 'encounter' battles shaped by the fog of war. Von Kluck still clung to the belief that the BEF had been destroyed and focused his attentions on Lanrezac's retreating Fifth Army. As previously noted, *First Army* was marching in a south-easterly direction. However, its right wing scraped against the BEF's rearguards on 1 September, resulting in violent clashes at Néry and Villers-Cotterêts.

## Action at Néry

Néry was a tiny French hamlet, most notable for the presence of a large ravine that lay to the east of the village, but a series of chance events caused it to become the site of a savage battle between British and German cavalry.

On the evening of 31 August the weary troopers of 1st Cavalry Brigade had arrived at the village seeking billets for the evening. The horsemen had spent several frustrating hours searching for a resting place and had arrived at Néry only after other options had been exhausted. Men, horses and officers were all tired. Unfortunately, the lateness of the hour of arrival and the tiredness of the brigade meant that normal security procedures were somewhat neglected.

The brigade was led by Brigadier General Charles Briggs, a hardened veteran who had made his name in the Boer War.

Unfortunately, Briggs made an uncharacteristic error and assumed that Néry was protected by other friendly troops. This was wrong. Néry actually lay in the middle of an undefended gap between 4th Division and II Corps. Worse still, unbeknownst to Briggs, German *4th Cavalry Division* was marching through the night to reach the village and exploit the opening.

A thick mist had descended over Néry in the early hours of 1 September. Visibility was so poor that orders to march at 4.00am were cancelled. Many soldiers took advantage of the delay to feed and water their horses. Several patrols were sent out into the foggy countryside to scout for enemy movement. All but one reported that the area was clear.

The one exception was a patrol led by 19-year old Lieutenant G.W.A. Tailby of the 11th Hussars. Tailby and his picked men found nothing on their initial sweep, but as they returned to the village they suddenly spotted a group of dismounted German cavalry. One of the British troopers fired a shot at the enemy, which prompted the Germans to mount up and charge after the scouting party. A life or death chase followed as the outnumbered hussars bolted back towards Néry. Tailby's horse tripped and fell, forcing the lieutenant to hide in some undergrowth until the Germans had ridden past. Fortunately, he was then able to remount and galloped back to warn 1st Cavalry Brigade of the danger that they faced. By now it was approximately 6.00am.

Unfortunately for the British, Tailby's news arrived too late. The young officer had only just finished giving his report when all hell broke loose. The Germans had deployed a dozen artillery pieces on the eastern side of the ravine, just 600 yards from Néry itself. At such close range, coupled with the fact that the Germans had achieved complete surprise, the results were simply devastating. Shells ripped through the village. Men caught in the open were struck down immediately, whilst the survivors sprinted for cover in buildings or behind walls. Lines of tethered cavalry horses were swept by shrapnel. One soldier recalled that the animals 'were terribly injured and killed and many of them had stampeded off with fright. There were men hanging onto them but we couldn't stop the horses bolting.'

Battery L of the Royal Horse Artillery was hit especially hard. The battery had been limbered up when the engagement began and was pounded by a hail of shells. Its commanding officer fell almost immediately and there were appalling casualties amongst horses and crew. Yelling orders over the roar of battle, second in command Captain Edward Bradbury managed to get three guns into action and desperately returned fire. It was an unequal contest. One gun was ripped apart by a direct hit and a second was reduced to cold silence when its crew was wiped out. Only Bradbury's gun stayed in action.

Lashed by shrapnel and rocked by high explosive blasts, Bradbury's gun team was soon reduced to just three men. Incredibly, the single gun returned fire for almost two hours. At around 8.00am the gallant Bradbury was mortally wounded by a shell that tore off both his legs. Another crewman recalled: 'Though the captain knew that death was very near, he thought of his men to the last, and begged to be carried away, so that they should not be upset by seeing him, or hearing the cries which he could not restrain.' Bradbury would receive a posthumous Victoria Cross for his courage. Surviving crewmen Sergeant Major George Dorrell and Sergeant Major David Nelson were also awarded the VC.

Bradbury's defiant two-hour stand had swung the tide of battle. The Germans had concentrated their fire on the single gun and given the British time to recover their senses. Brigadier General Briggs had reacted with typical aggression and organised a counterattack, sending units forward to turn the flanks of the German position. In some cases the British cavalry ran into German horsemen who were launching flank attacks of their own, provoking sudden close range fire fights. Mist still covered much of the battlefield and the fighting was confused and desperate. But the engagement inclined towards the British with every passing hour. Reinforcements were arriving on the scene. The 1st Middlesex arrived from the northwest. Battery I of the Royal Horse Artillery deployed alongside the wreckage of L Battery and poured punishing fire onto the German gun line.

By now the mist had lifted and the German position to the east of the ravine was left cruelly exposed. The plateau ceased to be a commanding position and became a death trap. The German gun line was swept by rifle and machine gun fire from the flanks and by shrapnel from the front. Under attack from all sides, the commander of *4th Cavalry Division* realised that retreat was the only option. British fire was so intense that eight of the German guns were left behind. The remaining four were subsequently found abandoned in nearby woodland.

What had begun as a disaster for the British had ended in a striking victory. *4th Cavalry Division* had been so badly mauled that its commander ordered it to scatter into its component parts to evade British pursuit. The action at Néry had effectively destroyed the formation and it would take several days to recover. German cavalry would not trouble the BEF for the remainder of the retreat.

**Action at Villers-Cotterêts**

Whilst 1st Cavalry Brigade was fighting for its life around Néry, Douglas Haig's I Corps was trudging through the dense forest of Villers-Cotterêts. It was a sweltering day and the woodland canopy amplified the heat, making the march a slow and tiring process. Rearguard duties fell to 4th (Guards) Brigade, under the command of Brigadier General Robert Scott-Kerr. The front line was held by the Irish Guards and 2nd Coldstream Guards. The Irish Guards had only been formed in 1900 and were therefore the youngest regiment of the army. This was to be their first major engagement.

At 6.30am German cavalry scouts tentatively approached the edge of the wood, only to be greeted a sudden fusillade of fire that drove them back in disorder. The Germans brought up infantry and artillery reinforcements and a running fight developed. The Guardsmen fell back to pre-designated positions and slowed the German advance with considerable skill. The British had the better of the early fighting. Scott-Kerr recalled: 'My impression of the German attack was that the infantry were doped. One saw groups of men walking up to our line mooning along with their rifles at the trail, as if stupefied.'

However, the situation changed around 10.00am when orders arrived informing the rearguard that they were expected to hold their ground until 1.00pm. According to Major George 'Ma' Jeffreys of the 2nd Grenadier Guards this order was given to allow time for the main body to halt and have a hot dinner! If so, it reflected a serious misunderstanding of the situation. The rearguard had enjoyed success in the morning due to its ability to fall back as necessary. The new order forced it to stand its ground in terrain that did not favour the defender. The dense undergrowth isolated men from their officers and thus seriously hampered command and control, as well as shortening fields of fire and diminishing the advantage enjoyed by the skilled British marksmen.

Unaware of the change in British orders, the Germans pressed forward. Enterprising groups of attackers worked their way through gaps in the British line and brought enfilade fire onto the defenders. Scott-Kerr, who was seriously wounded in the fighting, admitted that German machine guns were 'horribly efficient'. Jeffreys recalled that there was 'very confused fighting at point-blank range'. The rearguard suffered some 360 casualties in this period of bitter combat.

Fortunately for the British, the attackers were equally confused. It was impossible to gain an accurate picture of the action in the woodland and hard to maintain direction when bullets seemed to be flying in from every angle. The Germans declined to pursue 4th

(Guards) Brigade when the latter finally fell back from the forest in the early afternoon. Jeffreys commented that the Germans 'not only lost heavily but got very mixed up in the thick forest, and we could hear them shouting orders and blowing little horns apparently to rally their men.' The *Official History* noted that German prisoners reported being involved in several 'friendly fire' incidents during the battle.

The two small, bloody actions described above were the last major engagements of the Great Retreat. On the evening of 1 September, I Corps and II Corps were finally reunited. Although the weary soldiers of the BEF did not know it, the end of the epic march was fast approaching.

# Chapter 11: The End of the Retreat & the Battle of the Marne

The worst of the retreat was over. The first week of September was fearfully hot but the BEF could afford to make shorter marches, a small mercy that found a grateful audience amongst the men. The blistering pace of 24 and 25 August was no longer required.

James Edmonds recorded a French civilian's impression of the BEF as it marched past in early September: 'The soldiers, phlegmatic and stolid, march without appearing to hurry themselves; their calm is in striking contrast to the confusion of the refugees...as sportsmen who have just returned from a successful raid, our brave English eat with a good appetite, drink solidly, and pay royally those who present their bills...and depart at daybreak, silently like ghosts, on the whistle of the officer in charge.'

The army had changed. A fortnight of marching, fighting and short rations had hardened the soldiers. Between 23 August and 5 September the army had covered at least 200 miles. The BEF travelled light, having thrown away any impedimenta that the men judged useless. Shaving kits were one such item, and as a result many soldiers now wore beards. There were disturbing gaps in the ranks of some battalions, especially those of II Corps, but other units had seen no action whatsoever.

There were some causes for concern. Smith-Dorrien was worried that officer casualties had damaged army discipline and there were still thousands of stragglers limping along in the army's wake. Many battalions were jumbled up, with officers and men from different regiments forming ad-hoc groups. The Royal Artillery, still smarting from the loss of guns at Le Cateau, was increasingly concerned about the health of its overworked draught horses. Yet despite these problems, the BEF was unbroken. It had resisted all of von Kluck's attempts to destroy it and had survived a gruelling retreat in difficult conditions. It would soon play its role in turning the tide.

Meanwhile, important events were occurring on the wider front. *First Army* had overreached itself. Its flank was exposed to an attack from direction of Paris, where the newly formed Sixth Army was ready to spring into action. All across the front the German offensive was slowly but surely losing impetus. Officers and men were exhausted. Infantry boots were worn through and the cavalry was becoming immobilised for want of horseshoes. The rapid advance had stretched the German logistic network to its absolute breaking point. It could no longer supply the front line efficiently. On 4 September, Chief of the General Staff Helmuth von Moltke decided that the wheel in front of Paris had failed and ordered *First Army* and *Second Army* to hold their ground, whilst forces further east launched renewed offensives against the French.

The timing was disastrous for Germany. Joffre's counterstroke was almost ready and the delay gave him the time he needed to finalise his plans. He removed the sluggish and argumentative Lanrezac from command, replacing him with the dynamic Franchet d'Espèrey, thus ensuring that Fifth Army would be capable of playing a part in the coming battle. On 5 September, Joffre visited Sir John French to ask for British support in the Allied counterattack. Despite his agreement with Lord Kitchener, Sir John still harboured doubts about the viability of the operation and cooperation was by no means assured.

What followed was a moment of pure military theatre. Joffre addressed French directly, explaining the situation before declaring that he planned to throw every last man he had into the battle to save France. Building to a crescendo of emotion, he clutched Sir John's hands, imploring him to support the attack, closing by saying '*c'est la France qui vous supplie*' (it is France that begs you). The power of Joffre's appeal was overwhelming. Several witnesses reported the sight of tears on Sir John's cheeks. He attempted to reply, but the emotion of the moment and his difficulties with the language were too much. Instead he muttered, 'Damn it, I can't explain. Tell him that all men can do our fellows will do.' This was translated as a simple 'Yes'.

The BEF's retreat came to an end on 5 September. On 6 September the army turned and began to advance north. The movement came as a welcome surprise to many officers and men. Captain James Jack noted in his diary: 'This totally unexpected news almost passed belief after the long depressing retreat. This brigade is certainly in good form once more.'

The Battle of the Marne had begun. For the next week Allied forces would fight a confused, swirling engagement across a vast front. It was not a battle of sudden breakthroughs or dynamic manoeuvre. It was primarily a Franco-German clash, but the presence of the BEF was vital. Without Sir John's army a large gap would have been opened in the Allied lines and Joffre's counterattack would likely have failed before it had even begun. For the British, the fighting at the Battle of the Marne was minor compared to the harrowing experience of the Great Retreat. Total BEF casualties for the week-long Battle of the Marne were comparable to the losses suffered in a single day at the Battle of Mons.

Although the battle was confusing, there could be no doubt about the ultimate victor. The Germans were forced to retreat some 60 miles to north, ultimately halting on the line of the River Aisne. Paris was saved, and with it France. The German Schlieffen Plan had failed. There would be no swift victory in the west. The defeat caused Helmuth von Moltke to suffer a nervous breakdown. He is said to have reported to the Kaiser, 'Your majesty, we have lost the war.'

Germany was now locked into a vast two-front conflict that divided her armies and resources. Furthermore, the reckless decision to invade Belgium had arrayed the immense economic strength of the British Empire against Germany. Nevertheless, although the Battle of the Marne changed the tide of the First World War, it would still take four years of intense, bloody fighting before German forces were finally evicted from France.

# Conclusion: The Retreat to Victory

The British Army has a long history of starting its campaigns with a retreat. Before the First World War, Brigadier General Aylmer Haldane had undertaken a cycling tour in northern Spain, tracing the route used by Sir John Moore's army as it fell back to Corunna in 1808-1809. The tour gave Haldane confidence in 1914, for he felt that Moore's men had faced a far harder trial than the soldiers of the BEF. James Edmonds made similar comparisons when he wrote the first volume of the *Official History*. He argued that the retreat from Mons compared favourably with Moore's retreat to Corunna, the Duke of Wellington's retreat after Talavera in 1809 and the same general's move from Burgos to Ciudad Rodrigo in 1812. Edmonds was still alive in 1940 when the British Army was forced to make its desperate retreat to Dunkirk, and may well have compared the operation with his own experiences of 1914.

The army would come to look upon the Great Retreat of 1914 with a mixture of emotions. Many survivors recalled the crushing weariness caused by lack of sleep, long marches, and uncertain rations. Yet there was a degree of fondness for the experience, which stood in such stark contrast to the years of trench deadlock that followed. Cavalry officer George Barrow commented: 'I enjoyed every minute of the retreat – the excitement, the movement, the villages and fine old churches...' Others disagreed. Thomas Snow, who had commanded 4th Division in 1914, wrote soon after the war: 'the retreat of 1914 was not, as is now imagined, a great military achievement, but rather a badly bungled affair only prevented from being a disaster of the first magnitude by the grit displayed by the officers and men.'

Whilst there is undoubtedly an element of truth in Snow's assessment, subsequent authors have focused on the ultimate success of the withdrawal. Thrown into the maelstrom of battle, outnumbered by the enemy and supported by difficult and unreliable allies, the BEF not only survived but was then able to turn and fight in the decisive battle of the campaign.

Its success was attributable to a variety of factors. The advanced tactics and training of the army played a key role, as did the leadership of experienced junior officers. Crack British cavalry units were vital for screening the retreating footsloggers and were the unsung heroes of the retreat. Although there were several command level errors, the right decisions were made at key times. Smith-Dorrien's decision to stand at Le Cateau was fully justified, Robertson's idea of abandoning normal supply arrangements and leaving food stockpiles was inspired, and, even though it took Kitchener's intervention, John French was correct to support Joffre at the Battle of the Marne. There was also an element of luck. The failure of von Kluck to grasp the true position of the BEF hampered his pursuit and relieved the pressure at a crucial moment.

Historian John Terraine coined the phrase 'the retreat to victory', an apt summary that encapsulates the events of late August and early September 1914. The Great Retreat led directly to the decisive Battle of the Marne. Although this battle did not end the war, it dashed German dreams of a swift victory and gave Britain the time she needed to mobilise the immense resources of the Empire. Ultimately this process produced the large, well equipped and highly experienced British Army of 1918. This force would play a key role in driving the Germans from France, and in a strange twist of fate, the first and last British shots of the war were fired at the town of Mons. The BEF had come full circle.

# Select Bibliography

Ascoli, David, The Mons Star (Edinburgh, Birlinn, 2001)

Ballard, C.R., Smith-Dorrien (London, Constable & Co., 1931)

Barrow, George, The Fire of Life (London, Hutchinson & Co. Ltd, 1942)

Bird, Anthony, Gentlemen, We Will Stand and Fight: Le Cateau, 1914 (Ramsbury, Crowood Press, 2008)

Bloem, Walter, The Advance from Mons 1914 (Solihull, Helion & Co., 2011 reprint)

Bridges, Tom, Alarms and Excursions: Reminisces of a Soldier (London, Longmans, 1938)

Cave, Nigel & Sheldon, Jack, Le Cateau (Barnsley, Pen & Sword, 2008)

Craster, J.M., (ed.), Fifteen Rounds a Minute: The Grenadiers at War 1914 (London, MacMillan, 1976)

Edmonds, James, Official History of the Great War: Military Operations France and Belgium 1914, Vol.1, (London, Macmillan, 1923)

Gardner, Nikolas, Trial by Fire: Command the British Expeditionary Force 1914 (Westport, Praeger, 2003)

Haldane, Aylmer, A Brigade of the Old Army 1914 (London, E. Arnold, 1920)

Hamilton, Lord Earnest, The First Seven Divisions (London, Hurst & Blackett, 1916)

Hamilton, Richard F. and Holger Herwig, War Planning 1914 (Cambridge, Cambridge

University Press, 2010)

Herwig, Holger, The Marne 1914 (London, Random House, 2009)

Holmes, Richard, The Little Field Marshal: A Life of Sir John French (London, J. Cape, 1981)

Holmes, Richard, Riding the Retreat: Mons to the Marne Revisited (London, J. Cape, 1995)

Jones, Spencer, From Boer War to World War: Tactical Reform of the British Army 1902-1914 (Norman, University of Oklahoma Press, 2012)

Jones, Spencer, Stemming the Tide: Officers and Leadership in the British Expeditionary Force 1914 (Solihull, Helion & Co., 2013)

von Kluck, Alexander, The March on Paris and the Great Battle of the Marne 1914 (London, E. Arnold, 1920)

Lucy, John, There's a Devil in the Drum (London, Faber & Faber, 1938)

Murland, Jerry, Retreat and Rearguard 1914 (Barnsley, Pen & Sword, 2011)

Richards, Frank, Old Soldiers Never Die (London, Faber & Faber, 1933)

Scott, Peter, Dishonoured: The Colonels' Surrender at St. Quentin 1914 (London, Tom Donovan, 1994)

Sneddon, John Mason, The Devil's Carnival: 1st Battalion Northumberland Fusiliers August - December 1914 (London, Tommies Guides, 2012)

Spears, Edward, Liaison 1914: A Narrative of the Great Retreat (London, W. Heinemann, 1930)

Terraine, John, Mons: The Retreat to Victory (London, MacMillan, 1960)

Printed in Great Britain
by Amazon

74428569R00064